My Back Nine

Unleash Your Authentic Self

By Tony Caico

iUniverse, Inc.
Bloomington

My Back Nine
Unleash Your Authentic Self

iUniverse books may be ordered through booksellers or by contacting:

iUniverse
1663 Liberty Drive
Bloomington, IN 47403
www.iuniverse.com
1-800-Authors (1-800-288-4677)

Because of the dynamic nature of the Internet, any Web addresses or links contained in this book may have changed since publication and may no longer be valid. The views expressed in this work are solely those of the author and do not necessarily reflect the views of the publisher, and the publisher hereby disclaims any responsibility for them.

ISBN: 978-1-4502-7950-5 (sc)
ISBN: 978-1-4502-7951-2 (ebook)
ISBN: 978-1-4502-7952-9 (dj)

Printed in the United States of America

iUniverse rev. date: 12/23/2010

Dedicated from the bottom of my heart to my five phenomenal gifts from God: *AJ, Austin, Alexander, Andersen, and Annalise.* Throughout this journey, you guys have inspired me to shed my inauthenticity and rediscover myself. To have the opportunity to help shape your precious lives and teach you what I have learned lies at the core of my reason for existence.

Lord knows that each of you will struggle along the way at some point, but I will be there, guiding you every step of the way. I feel blessed by your presence in my life.

Contents

Introduction – The "TURN"

Imagine you're sitting down in the lounge at your favorite golf club. You have just finished playing the front nine, and you are enjoying a quick snack and a tasty beverage. Well, enjoying might be a stretch, considering the sparring match going on inside your head. You are at the turn, analyzing your first half performance and you soon realize that your thoughts have a very familiar tone. You came into today's round, like you always do, with certain expectations. You had a genuine sense of excitement in preparation for your golf match today. You started to think to yourself that maybe this is the day I shoot that ultimate score. Maybe, this is the day I get that elusive "hole in one". Maybe, this is the day I that I will just enjoy myself, relax, enjoy the company, enjoy the scenery, and just have a great time. Maybe, just maybe, this is the day that I will not get angry and lose my temper. Of course, then the front nine ends and you start wondering what went wrong. You realize that you have, once again, fallen short of your expectations. You begin carefully evaluating each hole and each shot that you have just played. You go through the excruciating exercise on how you could have shaved off four or five strokes on the front nine. Well, if you're anything like me, you have been through this painful evaluation hundreds of times. You know the drill; the little voice inside your head is replaying the entire front nine, and like I mentioned above, this replay has a very familiar tone. Usually, you question yourself, your decisions, your shot execution, and your overall play. The replay goes something like this:

"If I had only made that three foot putt on number two."

"Come to think of it, I really should have made both five foot putts on five and seven."

"I really should have chosen to hit a 4 iron off the tee on number six."

"Why can't I stay consistent with my pre-shot routine, like I do on the practice range?"

"Why do I always shoot the same score? I could have easily broken forty on the front nine."

"OK, relax, the front nine is over. The back nine is a new nine."

"It's OK, grab something cold to drink, a quick bite, and get ready for the back nine."

After I complete the first nine holes, these are the thoughts that usually occupy my mind each time I play this crazy game. Even if I have played well, my focus is usually on the improvements that I need to make on the back nine. The problem that I inevitably face is that my back nine is almost always a mirror image of my front nine. I typically make many of the same mistakes, even though I usually know what I have done wrong. Does this sound familiar to you? Do you sometimes wonder why things stay the same and your golf game really doesn't improve that much over time?

If you think about it carefully, the reason becomes crystal clear. Simply put, your deficiencies will continue to hinder your performance until you realize that your training, your preparation, and most importantly, your game plan needs improvement.

Your back nine performance will only improve if YOU improve. Not much different in real life, is it? Many of us are now realizing that we have made some crucial mistakes in the first half of our lives. At some point, usually around middle age, many of us come face to face with some sort of mid-life crisis. This crisis is usually accompanied by an underlying sense of insecurity that seeps into our pores and invades our space. Many of us feel that there is something missing, but we are not quite sure what it is that is causing this feeling of insecurity. What could it be?

Like our golf games, we really want to improve certain aspects of our lives, but we are not exactly sure what we should do or where we should start. We spend a lot of time thinking about our past, worrying about our future, and we wonder what we can change in order to make the back nine of our journey more rewarding and fulfilling than the front nine. Clearly, we all have varying levels of improvements we need to make, but for the most part, we all want to continue to get better and ultimately, be happier.

In golf terms, we all want to break that elusive ninety, eighty, or even seventy for the first time. We all want to cure our slice, our hook, our nerves, and all of the other bad habits that have hindered our performance on the front nine. We are starting to realize that in order to ensure that our back nine will improve; we really do need a better game plan, some better strategies, and a detailed and structured outline to help us reach our goals.

In a nutshell, that is what *My Back Nine* is all about. What do we need to do better to improve ourselves and truly enjoy the second half of our lives? The good news is that we have a major advantage over a simple golf match. The "turn" (or evaluation period) for us is the first step, and it can last as long as it takes to understand our past and get prepared for our future. We have time on our side. Time to analyze what happened in the early stages of our lives. Time to look at our conditioned behaviors, our past mistakes, our untimely decisions, and our true strengths and weaknesses. Time to really examine our front nine, the decisions we have made, and the paths we have chosen. Time to take a deep dive into our philosophic minds to find our true calling in life. After all, very few individuals find true happiness at a young age. It takes time, experiences, and deep self understanding to realize one's true potential. Many of us have to take the wrong path sometimes, to realize that it's the wrong path. The real question is what are we going to do about it? What are we going to change?

During this journey, we will take a close look at all of the key components of our lives. We will examine ourselves in an attempt to rebuild, rebound, and find our life's purpose. We will examine nine key individual components that make up our lives. Relationships, family, spirituality, health, career, and a few others that will help us identify the things we need to focus on to seek the inner peace we all strive for. *My Back Nine* will serve as a road map as you enter a different stage of your life. Clearly, the book title equates to a middle age life experience, but I believe this book can help people of all ages.

It's basically a "deep dive" into nine key areas of our lives, or the nine holes of our back nine.

So, why write a book about life and golf? What's the connection? The game of golf can be truly reflective of one's personality. Our ability to focus, prepare, practice, gain knowledge, and keep our composure are paramount to our success at golf. Are these not the same essential qualities we need to be successful in life? You bet they are, and we will use similar analogies throughout this book. Golf is a game that is very unique to each individual, and that is why there are so many different techniques, strategies, and levels of expertise. But this game has one thing in common with everyone, it is very personal. It's your game, your score, your slice (or hook). You own your golf game, like no other sport I have ever played. It is the most self-identifiable game that exists. It requires honesty, integrity, patience, intensity, and many other deep rooted human characteristics. That is if you choose to take it seriously, which is the way the game was meant to be played.

Many of us are on a soul-searching journey of our own these days, as we attempt to find our true "authentic golf swing". In Steven Pressfield's book, *The Legend of Bagger Vance*, he masterfully uses this reference as a metaphor for our continued search for our own "authentic self". We will talk more about this book (and movie), and draw upon other key references on the following golf holes in an attempt to draw comparisons between golf and life.

You may be thinking that since you do not play golf you might have difficulty understanding the analogies. Well, let me clear that up for you in a few sentences. For the edification of the non-golfers, let me briefly explain the concepts of the game of golf and how they relate to this book.

There are eighteen holes in a golf match. After playing the first nine holes (your front nine), most golfers take a break to have lunch (or a beverage of their choice). This is typically referred to as the "turn". It's a time to reflect on your front nine, and make plans to improve the next nine holes, or your back nine. This is the section of the book that you are reading now, our "introduction" if you will. A typical regulation eighteen hole golf course is broken down by the length of each hole, with each hole identified by a score called par.

Par is basically the amount of shots (or strokes) you have to get your golf ball in the hole. For those geometry majors, just consider this. A typical par 4 golf hole is 425 yards long. Par 4 means you can only hit the ball four times before you're expected to make it in the hole. Keep in mind that the hole is only about three times (in diameter) as big as the ball. Talk about difficult! Each nine hole section of a regulation golf course consists of two par 3 holes, two par 5 holes, and five par 4 holes. The pars 3's are the shortest, the par 4's a bit longer, and the pars 5's are the longest. Your final score is measured in relationship to par. So, if you add the nine holes above, your final score is measured against 36 (2 times 3 + 2 times 5 + 5 times 4) = 36. Basically, the sections in the book will be outlined like nine holes of the back nine, starting with #10. The par 3's will consist of shorter topics, the par 4's a bit more detailed and important, and the pars 5's are the top two critical holes on the golf course. All nine holes (or life components) are very important, but the importance will be outlined in descending order, from 5's, to 4's, to 3's. Additionally, each chapter will be introduced and framed similar to a description of a golf hole. For example, a sign on the golf course (or a detailed hole description) would state something like this:

"This hole is a dog-leg left (which means the hole goes left), there is water down the left side, and two bunkers on the right about 245 yards out. The green is surrounded by bunkers on the left, so keep your ball on the right side." I will use similar descriptions for each golf hole, outlining the key points of each life component. Also, each hole will be outlined according the number of strokes (key points on each topic) that we are allotted. In other words, the par 3's will usually have an outline consisting of three key points, the par 4's will have four key points, and the par 5's will have five. Just to make things more interesting, some of the golf holes will be completed below par.

So maybe you're asking yourself "where did this idea come from?" As you read through the following pages, you will see many items that are personally related to me. To illustrate each life component, I use my own front nine life experiences and my ideas, goals and plans for my back nine as the framework of each hole. After all, the entire premise for *My Back Nine* came to me in a very unusual manner, and at a very interesting point in my life. Over the last several years, a series of mistakes, poor choices, and a few uncontrollable events propelled me into a deep depression. My marriage started falling apart, I lost the best job I ever had, had a few other personal and financial tragedies, and in the end, lost everything. My house went into foreclosure, I was out of work for the first time in my life, I was no longer with my children each day, and I was so deeply depressed I couldn't get out of my own way. My life was a complete mess, and I hit rock bottom. I had nothing left, materially anyway. I will dive deeper into my past throughout the book, but the events above were the culmination of an already declining life situation for me. You see, my front nine was mired with bad choices and mistakes. Over spending, over indulging, making bad decisions, and living with an over-sized ego were just a few of the contributors. In golf terms, I had a bad slice, I played golf courses I couldn't afford to play, I bought clubs that were too expensive, I was a horrible golf partner with a bad attitude, and I cheated. It's funny, even though I used the golf references to frame the prior sentence; these golf analogies were also true of me on the golf course. I didn't even realize it until I finished writing this, just now. Wow, this is great. It really feels good to admit faults, but only if you are willing to do something about it. Well, I am ready, and I suppose you are as well, which is why you have picked up this book.

The series of events in the early part of 2008 were really just the "straws that broke the camel's back" for me. I was out of work for what seemed like forever, and wasn't even close to being in the frame of mind to get a good job. Even in my state of depression, my ego was still way too large to take just any job. After all, I was the director of sales for the entire eastern half of the U.S. for a division of a major worldwide banking institution. Unemployment was something that happened to "other people," certainly not me. Well, there I was, out of work, losing confidence, and wallowing in self pity. After months of basically not doing anything, I took the only job I could get, as a bartender, something I had prior experience with, only "twenty years ago!" Needless to say, things were pretty bad and getting worse by the day. I was drinking, still making bad decisions, and still very depressed. I never imagined that rock bottom was a place for me, but there I was. So what to happened to me, what changed?

On Friday morning June 27th, at about 2a.m., I awoke from a deep sleep with three words ringing in my head, *"My Back Nine."* A series of thoughts started rushing through my brain. I couldn't contain these thoughts, so I got up out of bed, went to my computer, and started writing the introduction to this book. Many of the lines you are reading right now were written that night. I wrote about five paragraphs, and plotted out a rough outline of the nine components that, in my view, would make up the key facets of one's life. Especially the second half on one's life. Actually, at the time, I was only thinking of my life. Therein lies the theme and title *"My Back Nine."* I did all of this in about an hour, and then fell into the best deep sleep I have had since I can remember. Here's how I remember it. *"Tony, you are 45 years old, and god willing you will live until you are ninety. You are at the exact mid-point of your life. You are getting ready to head into the second half, or the back nine of your time on this earth. Now tell me, what are you going to do to actually change, and make your back nine better? What major life components are important to you, and how will you improve on these components to help you rebuild and regain all of the things you have lost? What is most important in your life, what mistakes did you make on the front nine, and how will they effect your decision making on the back nine?"*

That is it, my friends. This single premise and series of thoughts have literally changed my life. Was it God? I am sure it was now. I have since renewed my faith and have become more spiritual than I have ever been, and I can't get my hands on enough reading material on spirituality. Since that night, my life and my attitude have really changed. The next morning I just felt different. I had some kind of bounce back in my step. Everything had changed. My attitude, my focus, my outlook, and my desire, just like that. I went to the kitchen to get some cereal from the cabinet and grabbed the first one I could get my hands on. It was a box of LIFE cereal. I looked at the box, and all over the cereal box, were messages for me, I couldn't believe it. Messages like *"embrace your life,", "make the most of rainy days,", "reach new heights," "look at life in a new way."* The cereal box was actually talking to me. Crazy, right? I was really starting to feel good, alive for the first time in months. After breakfast, I went to my computer to start my daily Internet job search. I opened up my portfolio, and right there, staring at me, was a business card that said "Invent your Life." You see, a few months back I was in the gym, working out, when I noticed a business card for a life coach. I thought to myself, "If anyone needs a life coach, it's you, Tony." I took the card, but never called. I was even too depressed to seek help, which I assume happens to many people in the state of depression. But today was different, I owned this day, it was my day to call this person. So, I did. We made an appointment for a few days later. After I met with my new life coach, I knew that this was going to be really good for me. I starting thinking about the unbelievable synergies between what my new life coach did for a living, and all the things that I love to do best. I love to read, to write, to talk, to learn, to influence, and most of all, I love to help others. After that first meeting, my new course was charted. I was going to get on a twelve month plan to get my life back on track, I was going to start writing this book (pretty cool, right?), and then I was going to start using all of my new found focus and energy to set a new course for my life. I was finally starting to see a light at the end of the tunnel, and felt that I could actually take back control of my life. I finally realized the incredible vibrational pull that comes when you let go of the noise in your mind, separate yourself from your circumstances, and prepare yourself for what is meant to be. Freeing your mind from your old habits and baggage is truly the key to unlocking your full potential. I have a story to tell, and I have a strong desire to help others. This, I believe, is my calling, my true path so to speak. AWESOME, I have finally figured it out. You see, there is a path for everyone. There is a reason for our existence. God put us all here to do something unique, something special. The fundamental question is "Will you take advantage of your God-given talents and do something significant with your life?" The path is sometimes hard to see, as our vision gets blurred over the years, but it's always there. Some of us just take longer to figure out which path is right for us. I am quite sure that I am not the only one who has had difficulty finding their way. I have had countless conversations with friends and colleagues that have gone through similar struggles in their life, especially at the midpoint of their lives.

My front nine and first half life experiences and mistakes will provide an excellent reference point for me to figure out what "not to do" and which path "not to take" on my back nine journey. I feel that this is a natural progression for me, because without those bad choices I would have never gotten to this point, and you fine folks wouldn't be reading this book.

A few weeks after my new found enlightenment, I actually found new employment. You see my attitude was changing, my thinking was changing, and the sun was coming out every day. I really started thinking that everything was starting to turn in my favor, and it was. A long way to go still I thought, but I'm on my way to leading a more fulfilling and authentic life.

That's the goal here, folks. To identify with our true self, and to make the necessary adjustments on each key life component (or golf hole) on our back nine. It's time to get the machete out and clear our path. Are you ready?

OK, my friends, we have just taken our break, and completed the turn. We have enjoyed our tasty beverage, got a little bite to eat, and we are ready to tackle the back nine. I hope as you read through this introduction you were thinking about your own personal story. The mistakes you have made and the things that you want to do to improve during the second half of your own lives. As we go through the next nine holes, we will take the time to look back into our past in order to get our footing for the present, and set the right course for our future. Don't worry; we will go through this back nine together, shot by shot. We will face water hazards, sand bunkers, high winds, trees, and many other obstacles along the way. We will learn together how to overcome these obstacles, and in the end, we will each find our one true swing, and our one true self. So, go ahead, get in your golf cart, keep your feet in, push the pedal down, and by all means, enjoy the ride.

"Trust the process, Embrace the journey, and Transform your life" — Darren Gee

#10 – "Your Ultimate Foursome" – Par 5

"Home is one place in this entire world where hearts are sure of each other. It is the place of confidence. It is the place where we tear off that mask of guarded and suspicious coldness which the world forces us to wear in self-defense, and where we pour out the unreserved communications of full and confiding hearts. It is the spot where expressions of tenderness gush out without any sensation of awkwardness and without any dread of ridicule"

— Frederick W. Robertson

On the course *- We start our back nine with a very challenging par 5. There are many hazards on this long par 5, including trees, water, and sand. The first hole of the back nine is very important to our overall journey. We have just analyzed our front nine performance, and now it's time to improve our golf shots and ultimately finish the round with a solid score. Yes, this will be very difficult. However, if you are prepared to make the necessary swing adjustments on each shot, the results can be very favorable.*

Before we begin this back nine journey together, it's critically important that I stop right here and make a point. The introduction or "the turn" of this book is mandatory reading. The introduction provides the framework for this entire endeavor. As a matter of fact,

1

"the turn" is where it all begins for many of us. It's the moment in time that we realize we need something different in our lives. When we feel that we are ready to face our past, put it behind us, and truly learn to live in the present in an attempt to create the future of our dreams. It can be something very small, like adjusting a few small items to make our lives better. Or, something much larger in proportion, like changing everything and completely altering our lifestyles. For me, it's been the latter, a complete transformation and life changing experience. You and I will play this back nine together, but before we do, you must read the introduction. If not, the overall journey and experience will not make near as much sense. OK, enough preaching, grab your driver (or club of choice) and let's tee it up!!

Stroke 1 - Family

Why is Family one of the nine key life components? On the surface the answer to this question seems fairly easy to figure out, but most likely, it has a different meaning and associated priority for each individual. I started with family because this is where it all starts, where we all came from, our mother's womb. Without Mom (and yes, Dad) none of us would even be here. As we start our back nine journey together, what could be a better place to begin than with family? After all, our family situations and circumstances provide the underlying background for everything that we were, are, and endeavor to become. Regardless of the relationship you have with your family today, I am sure that you will all agree that these are the most important relationships of all. Maybe they are not important in your life right now, but they probably should be.

For me, this is certainly true. My family relationships are broken, and up until now, I spent more time focusing on other (less important) relationships that were easier to manage. That's why we are here, my friends, to examine together, everything in our lives. To stop taking the "easy way out," and to start to unveil the reasons why certain parts of our lives just don't work. To do this, we will need a very intense "mirror check." Throughout this entire book, we will be looking very closely at ourselves. This is especially important as we identify the broken pieces of our lives, and more specifically, our family relationships. There is an old expression that comes to mind: "you can't choose your family." That is a true statement, but you can choose what you do with your family relationships. This is very hard for many people; it was certainly hard for me.

However, if we truly wish to improve our lives on the back nine, we must concentrate on improving the relationships with our family members. We will talk more about relationships in general on #16, but relationships with our families we will talk about now, on this critical par 5. As indicated in our introduction (which I know you read), the two par 5's (Family and Spirituality) are the two most important golf holes we will play on this back nine. As we pave our way through this material on family, I would like you to start thinking about your own family and each individual family relationship. What are the relationships that work, and why? Which relationships do not work, and why? This is a great place to begin. To assist you with this process, let me set the stage by talking about my own family. I have five children (yes, that's not a typo), a mother and father (still alive, thank God), two sisters and one brother. I have two half brothers and a half sister from my dad's first marriage, and a litany of nephews, nieces, aunts, uncles, and cousins. I am divorced, so I have an ex-wife as well. She is definitely still part of my family and always will be. We have five wonderful children together, and our focus has always and will always be on these five gifts from God. Unfortunately, all of my grandparents have passed on.

I will tell you that as of right now, other than the relationships I have with my children, I am not at all satisfied with any of my other family relationships. That's right, not a single one. Some are better than others, some don't exist at all, but improvements are needed throughout. Many of you may be in the same boat. Again, that is why we are here. To examine why these relationship are broken, and to determine what we can do to make them better. More on these relationships later on this hole, specifically on stroke four.

This is very important material here, but don't worry, we will work through this together. In order to clear our path for the other eight holes on the back nine, the family section really needs to be examined. I realize that this will be more challenging and/or painful for some than for others, but I don't think anyone can truly have a successful life journey (first half or second half) without a detailed game plan that includes a strong focus on the family.

> ***Back on the course***. *That was a very admirable tee shot on the first hole, and a very good start to our back nine. In order to have a successful golf match, we must keep a positive attitude, and stay focused on each individual stroke. When we hit a good shot, we need to remember what we just did, and repeat it on the next shot. Successful golfers refer to this as "muscle memory," something that will help us keep the ball in the "short grass."*

Stroke 2 – Childhood

In order to properly examine our front nine experiences, it's important to go as far back as we can. Again, this will be more difficult for some than others. For me, it's very difficult. My memory is very foggy when it comes to my childhood. I can remember bits and pieces, but have a very hard time remembering events, times, places, and the details of anything that happened before the age ten or so. In contrast, I have a friend who can vividly explain things that happened to her when she was four and five years old. I believe that the more you can remember about your childhood, the more prepared you are to enter adulthood. I would say that my poor childhood memory has been a deterrent to me maturing throughout my life, and this is one of the reasons it has taken me longer than most to find myself. I can say this now because of the self examination phase I am going through.

This is a phase that I am actually still in as I write this book, and the phase that many of you may be going through as well. After all, many of you may have been attracted to this book because you realize that self examination is exactly what you need. That is awesome, and a great first step. You see, I am totally comfortable with the fact that I didn't realize many of these things until now. I say this because I think there are many people who will never figure it out. These people will just "jelly-fish" through life, without ever understanding their true path and/or life purpose. That may be OK for some. But not for me, and I presume, not for you either.

Let me briefly explain what I do remember from my childhood. As I go through the next few sentences, please be cognizant of your own childhood. The things you remember, the things you wish you could forget, and the reason why analyzing them now is a critical component to our back nine success.

I grew up on Long Island, New York, in the early seventies. From what I can remember, my childhood was very normal. We lived primarily in middle class neighborhoods, and I grew up in a very safe atmosphere, going to school, playing with friends, and playing tons of sports. Although my early memory is weak, I can usually define these times by the sports I played. My dad (Italian) was a salesman and my mom (Irish) a homemaker. Keep this in mind, as it will come up again when we talk about conditioned behaviors later on this hole, as we get closer to the green. I was raised with three siblings, and older brother and sister, and a younger sister. We were Catholic like most of the families where we lived. Another item that will come up again, when we discuss spirituality on #14. I went to school, played almost every sport known to man, and for the most part, had a very happy and normal childhood. My parents did the best they could, I am sure of it. Back in those days, you were to discipline your children, attempt to get them on the right track spiritually, and do your best to teach them right from wrong. I am confident that my parents tried to do all of those things the best they knew how, and I am thankful to them for their efforts. When was the last time I told them? Now, that's a different story. Probably, today, after I finish writing this section. That's the thing about writing, reading, and self discovery. You actually grow and change while you are doing it. It's working for me, how about you?

As you read this you may be saying, "Well, that childhood experience is not very interesting." Well, it becomes more interesting the deeper you dive. Here's what I mean. Through my own careful examination, I thought to myself, how could I have strayed so far off course, when my childhood was so normal? What was I missing? Where did I go wrong? When did I go wrong? Well, as we dig deeper into our past, we are sure to uncover some "trigger" points that will help us explain why we choose the paths we choose.

Back then, there wasn't much of focus on communication. There weren't many alternative sources of information for parents, no Internet, no self-help books, just conditioned behaviors that were passed down from their parents. I can only assume at this point that my parents never really knew or understood me once I reached a certain age, and much of that continues to this day with them as well as other family members. The fact that I don't remember much about those years, in my view, is a direct correlation to the lack of information and the lack of communication. This is actually really good news for us. We have much better tools than our parents did; and we have access to more information. Therefore, we should be better equipped to improve communication with our children, and this should help us (and them) lead more fulfilling lives. Just to be clear, I am not saying that my parents didn't do a good job raising me or my siblings. That is not the case. As I mentioned above, I'm sure they did the best they knew how given the available tools and information at their disposal. So, as we look back on our own childhood, let us try and remember all of the good times. Surely, we all had good times. I can certainly remember my first touchdown, my first home run, and my fist twenty point basketball game. I also remember having fun with my siblings, playing outside with friends, going on long trips to Florida, and really never being concerned about having a roof over my head or food on the table.

I remember that my dad was at every ball game I played, and there were a ton of games. I remember how my mom was always so loving, supportive, and affectionate with me and my siblings. These are the things you can draw upon when you grow up, when these relationships get strained and go downhill. For me, the foundation was there, and that is something that has always been with me.

On the other hand, if your childhood was mired with disappointment, hurt, and pain, there are ways to deal with that as well. If you haven't talked through these things with someone, than that is the first step. I have recently discovered that talking about your pain is extremely liberating. Remember, everyone has pain, and everyone has a story. Unfortunately, not everyone is willing to admit their mistakes and/or face their pain. I would venture to guess that the fine folks reading this book do not fall into that category. After all, we are working on self improvement, and that is an awesome feeling. Right?

> **Back on the course**. *OK, you guys are doing great on this opening hole. Your ball is in the middle of the fairway, and you are ready to take your third shot. Let's stay dialed in, as there are still many obstacles in our way on this difficult par 5.*

Stroke 3 - Family History - Conditioned Behaviors

Just to clarify, the family history I will refer to in this section relates to your childhood and teenage years. The time of your life where you actually learn how to be who you are, or so you think. As we get older and wiser, we start to realize that we really didn't know near as much as we thought we knew. Heck, I just turned forty five years old and I have learned more about myself in the past two years than I have in the last ten.

Our teenage years are the time in our lives where we develop ideas, behaviors, and opinions on almost every topic. This is the basic framework that has shaped our lives up until now. We can call this time the "SpongeBob Squarepants" stage. My kids will love that. The stage of our lives where we are literally sponges, absorbing every bit of information our brains can handle.

Human beings are creatures of habit by nature. We learn from what we see, hear, and experience. In order for us to realize our true potential, we must examine all of our conditioned behaviors, both good and bad. We then need to determine if these behaviors are still good for us, or if they have run their course. After all, many of the behaviors we learn at a young age (or any age) are very good for us, and have helped shape our lives in a very positive manner. It's very important that we focus on the good things, as well as the not so good things as we take this journey. It's very beneficial to have a "frame of reference" (both positive and negative) so we can decipher what we will do (or change) in our attempt to improve our individual situations. This is a very difficult proposition for many people, because it sometimes takes a while for us to actually figure out whether the conditioned behavior is good or not. As we grow and mature, our lives change, our thoughts change, and most importantly, our understanding of things change. As we evolve, we learn more about ourselves, our strengths and weaknesses, and why we have them. What we find is that our understanding of our behaviors elevates as we mature, and sometimes that means the things we thought were good for us are actually not so good.

If you recall a few pages back, I said I would come back to the fact that my dad was an Italian salesman. I will use this as an example to point out conditioned behaviors (both good and bad) that I learned just by the sheer nature of what my father did for a living as well as his nationality. Through no fault of his, I developed both positive and negative behaviors just by being the son of an Italian salesman. My dad was a salesman for an oil company, a job that sounds pretty darn good right now. I remember him working very hard, and for all intents and purposes, we always had what we needed throughout childhood. In turn, I also became a very hard worker and a very successful salesman and sales manager. The subject came up in conversation from time to time, but I never really thought that much about the fact that my dad pretty much had the same job as I did. As I look back on my career, my hard work, my ability to sell, and my leadership qualities provided me the fuel that I needed to propel me to a very successful career thus far. On a side note, my hitting rock bottom had absolutely nothing to do with my skill, work habits, or sales results. Those were all really good things in my life, and I can now say that this was learned behavior instilled in me by my father. With all due respect to my mother, she actually ran her own successful real estate business after we were older. So, the work ethic was there and instilled in me from both parents. Good conditioned behaviors, for sure.

Now for the not so good part. My dad was also Italian, and very proud of his heritage, as he should be. From a very young age, I identified strongly with being Italian, and for some reason, developed a private, yet powerful obsession with the Italian mob. I remember watching *The Godfather* for the very first time, and thought to myself, "wow, these guys are really cool." That was it, I was hooked. Over the years, the movies kept coming. *Godfather II* and *III*, *Casino*, *Mobsters*, and my all time favorite; *Goodfellas*. These guys got whatever they wanted. They just took it. They had money, power, women, they gambled, and just had tons of fun, or so it seemed to me. They were also portrayed as "so called" family men. They had wives and kids, went to church, and to me, had a pretty cool life.

Don't worry; I am not going to confess to any murder, theft, or any illegal activity. I have made some poor choices throughout my adult male life, but breaking the law was never my thing. However, I did learn some very bad behaviors just because I identified so strongly with being an Italian mobster. It actually became the role I played in my "fabricated and egotistical" mind. This roll took on a life of its own as my business career skyrocketed and I started gaining notoriety and having more success. Low and behold, not that I need any more encouragement, but my favorite Italian "role model" of all time came on the scene, Tony Soprano. He even had the same name as I did. Of course, so did Tony Montana, another character (although not Italian) that I identified with immediately. I never missed an episode of *The Sopranos*, and I strongly identified with the main character. Heck, the writers even gave Tony's son the same name I gave my son, A.J. During this ego-laden phase of my life, many friends and colleagues quite often referred to me as Tony Soprano, and boy did that play right into my hands. I loved and cherished the role, but in the end, I learned some hard lessons. Heavy drinking, intimidation, posturing, drugs, womanizing, and gambling all became a large part of my life at a young age, and that pattern continued for many years. Unfortunately, for me, I rarely got "caught" doing anything. I lived with this huge ego and a Teflon shell around me, and thought "that nothing could ever happen to me." Boy was I wrong.

Bottom line, this was definitely bad conditioning. Something that I think I always knew, but I just was never ready or willing to come to grips with the fact that what I was doing was not only infantile, but it was really hurting the people closest to me, my family.

So, let's bring this full circle. Again, as you were reading my story, I hope you were thinking about your own childhood and teenage years, and what you identified with. What are your conditions behaviors? How have they affected your life? Are they still affecting your life? The key here is to dive deep into what behaviors are good for you, and which ones are bad for you. Deep down inside, at any point in time, we should know which ones are good and which one are not. My examples above were easy to identify as good and bad, right? So, why did I continue the bad behavior? Because I wasn't ready to change for the better.

I was resistant to changing my behaviors, because I identified with them, I was having too much fun, and they became part of who I was. You see your identity and ego (and mine was large) can take over your life if you're not careful. That is exactly what happened to me. The character I made up in my mind through my conditioned behaviors actually came to life. *I was Tony Soprano.* I had a wife, a family, and went to church every Sunday. The whole nine yards. I hid behind the confines of being a respected family man and successful business man. Behind the scenes, mostly on my own, I kept feeding my demons. I knew what I was doing was wrong the entire time, and now I am actually thankful to have lost it all. If I didn't, I may have never found my way. After my recent epiphany, it all started making sense to me. I eventually realized that I wasn't really that person obsessed with the mob and making poor choices; that was just a character I created. This character is gone now, and that's good news for me, my five awesome kids, and everyone else in my family and in my life.

The bottom line is to stay focused on yourself and the things around you. If you do, you can break the mold of poorly conditioned behaviors (or the framework we mentioned above). Some examples of poor conditioning could include: family heritage, bad temper, poor communication, lack of affection, alcohol and drug abuse, poor eating habits, self-esteem issues, mental, physical, or sexual abuse, and lack of attention. I'm sure there others that many of you have experienced. Regardless of what they are for you, if you haven't identified and/or dealt with these conditioned behaviors, now is the time. As I mentioned earlier, it may be a good idea to seek professional help in an attempt to uncover the reasons for your bad conditioning. Either way, it's critical that to attack this now. Now is time for us to investigate, understand, and release many of the behaviors that have hindered our performance on the front nine.

Behaviors that we know shouldn't be a part of our lives. Take it slow, take these one at a time, and learn to accept, understand, and ultimately let go. Accomplishing these tasks will be hard, but very necessary to changing your life for the better.

Back on the course. You guys are doing really well on this hole. I told you it would be a challenge, and we are not out of the woods yet. Actually, we were never in the woods. Our tee shot was in the fairway, our second shot right down the middle, and our third shot has hit the green. However, the green on this hole is very large and has many breaks and variations. Our golf ball has landed on the front right side of the green, but the hole is on the back left. We will have to carefully navigate these last two strokes in order to get our par.

Stroke 4 - Family Relationships

Many of you may want to avoid this section, but we know that we can't. Let's face it; we have been putting this off for a long time. Now, I will not presume that after you read this section all of your family relationships will be better. However, the thought process that goes through your mind while you read this section will likely provide the jolt that you need to improve your family relationships.

This includes spouses (or significant other), children, parents, siblings, and extended family members. Now, you may be saying, why should I be focused on all of these relationships? Shouldn't I just worry about the close family relationships? Well, that is a very good question. What I will tell you is that ALL of these relationships are important. Clearly, some of these relationships are more important than others. The main focal point here is to tap into what is important for YOU.

For me, this is really huge. As I mentioned before, my relationships with my children are fantastic. I am struggling a little with my two older boys, but we are starting to find our groove again, and it gets better each day. As for my other family relationships, they all need improvements. Throughout my recent transformation, I realized that I have many family members that I don't even know. I actually have two half brothers and a half sister that I haven't seen in years. Not to mention two immediate sisters and one brother that I would like to know better. While I was contemplating this chapter, I thought to myself, I have spent many hours cultivating relationships with people (all over the country), but I have not done the same with my own family. Again, that's just me. Some can use the excuse that they don't have enough time, or that these people don't really want relationships with me. That may be true, but wouldn't you feel better if you made the attempt? Do you ever wonder how valuable new family relationships can be in your life? Of course you do, everyone does. So, what are you going to do about it? You will have to figure out what is vital and important to you in your life. After all, that is what this back nine journey is all about. What things will we change in the second half of our lives to improve in all categories? Family is a good place to start.

Regardless of your age, reconnecting with family members can be a very rewarding experience. Take some time and make a list of family members you have not seem or talked to in a while. Think about how you might feel reconnecting with these family members. What you might find, is that they feel the same way you do. Where does the time go? What have you been up to? Tell me about your family? There a million things you can talk about, write about, etc. With the addition of Facebook and other sources, reconnecting is easier than it has ever been. Think about how that will make you feel. Believe me, it feels really good. I have done it already, and I am working my way through in an attempt to reconnect with many of these great people that, in my view, should be a part of my life. The first thing I did was to ask my parents to give me all of the names and numbers for all of their relatives. That was a great first step, and they were very happy and had a sense of pride that I wanted to take the time with their respective sides of the family. With that list, I was able to get the contact information for most of my relatives. My goal will be to get the rest of the contact numbers from the relatives on the list. There is an old saying, "Where there is a will there is a way". How very true that statement is, and it is truly liberating to set such an important goal and than work to achieve that goal. This was also an ice-breaker that I used to improve the relationship with my parents.

Now, let's talk about your parents. This includes step-parents as well. Clearly, this may be difficult for many of us, especially the Baby Boomer generation. You see, as I mentioned before, communication was much different when we grew up than it is now. Many times, we have a hard time connecting with our parents. However, at some point and time we must take responsibility for these relationships. While you read these words, think about all of the things you want to say to your parents.

Self evaluation and self improvement is very hard work, but you must consider the fact that you probably have better tools in place to improve these relationships than your parents do. That is not a slight on them, it's just that we have much more information available to us these days, and more available knowledge tends to lead towards more emotional availability and better communication skills. Just think how good you will feel when your relationship with your parents improves because of your hard work and dedication. We spend so much time focused on ourselves, our careers, and other items, and we tend to lose focus on the people that brought us into this world. Trust me, I certainly fell into this category, and I am going to try and rebuild right along with you.

As I mentioned before, I am taking this journey with you. I have already started to reconnect with my parents. Actually, it has come very easily for me because my parents have really been there for me throughout my recent depression and series of unfortunately events. What I realized is that the tables turned on me, and instead of me being the big shot and taking care of everyone else, my parents (and other family members) were there to help me out of some sticky situations. As a matter of fact, as I sit here and write this, I am residing in a home that my sister owns. Through the kindness and generosity of my sister and her husband, I have a better chance to get back on my feet. Although, it's hard for me to say, this means so much to me, and I am eternally grateful. It took me quite some time to come to grips with this, as accepting things from others has been a slow and painful process. But I soon realized that they were there to help me, and this has helped fuel my desire to rebuild relationships with them. It has been difficult due to the communication barriers, but I am determined. Contrary to what many people say, you are NEVER told old and it's NEVER too late.

The sincere effort and dedication to meeting your goals and improving your relationships, that's what counts. Remember, this is your back nine and you will not be denied.

Now let's talk about your children, providing you have them. Everyone's situation is different, but I would venture to say that your relationships with your children are the absolute most important of all. For sure, it's that way for me. I feel so very blessed and fortunate to have five children, but like most of us, I have some major improvements to make regarding parenting. I made a series of life choice mistakes, and those mistakes have cost me dearly, mostly because I have lost some critical time with my children. Fortunately, for me, my children are still very young and I have time to make things right. My relationships with them improve every day, and they are the joys of my life.

I have two fantastic books that I have used, and continue to use to assist me in being a better father. One is *The Father's Almanac*, by S. Adams Sullivan. This book covers the gamut, from early development, right through the teenage years. It's one of those books that will never go out of style. I received this book as a gift after my first son (A.J.) was born in 1994.

I will be honest and tell you that I thumbed through, read a few chapters about how to take care of babies, and put it on my bookshelf. Over the years, I have perused through it on occasion, but never gave it the attention it deserves. I have since read through the entire book, and the first thing that I realized was that I have already made a plethora of mistakes. Well, I can't do anything about that now. But, hey, I am on the back nine now, and my focus has changed.

Like I said, I am fortunate that my kids are still young, and I can still take advantage of all of the new tools I am learning. The contents of this book are amazing. Things like:

- Teaching and Discipline – self-esteem, setting goals, instructions, role modeling

- Learning with your children – music, arts and crafts, computer, sports, geography, etc…
- Playing with your children – ball games, toys, video games, horsing around, laughing
- Working with your children – outdoors jobs, indoor jobs, chores (allowance), cooking

Regardless of what age your kids are, it's never too late to teach them something. One thing I have realized is that they are "always watching."

Another great book is *Raising a SON*, by Don and Jean Elium. This book is obviously geared towards boys. One of my college friends sent this to me after the birth of my second son. Little did he know at the time that I would have two more boys. Yes, that is four in total, in case you missed that before. Anyway, this book is awesome and has truly helped me understand what makes boys unique and really what makes them tick. It also has a "cradle to career" theme, and provides a series of tools to help parents throughout the entire process of raising boys. Similar to the first book, I never made it all of the way through this book until just this year. I have found some precious "gems" reading this book, and they have already helped me with my sons. The bottom line to this publication is that boys turn into men, and men are made, not born. That is an awesome responsibility, but one I am proud to have as a father of four growing boys.

As I indicated earlier, I am divorced, and do not see my kids everyday. That has been difficult to say the least, but the time I do spend with them has become so much more rewarding than it used to be. I would venture to guess that I am more "present" in my children's lives now that I ever was when I actually lived with them. Don't get me wrong, I still feel sever pain not being able to tuck my kids in to bed every night. But I can tell you that I do my very best to spend quality time with them when we are together. When it comes to my back nine journey, the time I get to spend with my children outweighs anything that I will discuss in this book. As I mentioned above, I have four boys. I also have a daughter, who is the youngest. What a blessing it has been for me to have a little girl. She has brought so much joy to my life; I can't imagine life without her. Tea parties, haircuts, ear piercings, and other little things are so very different with my daughter than with my sons. Although she is only four, my relationship with her continues to grow, and I feel very grateful that God has blessed me with a daughter.

Regardless of what age your children are, have you recently thought about what you would like to change? Not in them, in you. Remember, this is your back nine, not theirs. Your responsibility lies within your desire to change, your desire to make things better, and to connect deeper with your children. The good news is that you can utilize the same skills with your children that you used with you parents. These are same skills that you used (or will use) to reconnect with those distant family members.

Communication, sincerity, dedication, focus, determination, and most importantly, LOVE. What you will find is that once you make a commitment to improve, you will improve. Just get started. Make a list of the things you would like to improve. I want to spend more time with them, I want to learn more about what my child likes; I want to spend time teaching them the things I know. Once you start down this path, you will figure it out. At the end of this path are rewards that you will cherish for a lifetime, and rewards they will cherish for a lifetime. Because of you they'll gain rewards they will be able to pass on to their children. What a great feeling. Just think about it, by improving your relationships with your parents, your siblings, your relatives, and your children, generations of people down the line will be impacted. Your life is that important and your back nine will resonate with many people for years to come.

Back on the course*. What a nice putt. Your short-game (which includes putting) is probably the most important part of your overall game. If you are a good chipper and putter, you can shave many strokes off your game. Obviously, you are a good putter, so the conclusion of each chapter should come easy for you. In this case, the family relationship "putt" was very difficult, but your putt has landed right next to the hole. All that is left is for you is a tap in putt. Be sure to take your time, because these short putts can be missed.*

Stroke 5 – Family Summary - Past, present, future

In order for us to stay targeted and focused on our family, it's critical that we use the past as our "frame of reference" and the PRESENT to make our improvements. If you identify clearly with what has gone on in the past, and you make the necessary adjustments in real time, the future will take care of itself. A former mentor of mine used to say "take care of the means, and the ends will take care of themselves." Be careful not to spend too much time on the past, and you should probably spend less time thinking about the future.

The present moment is really all that matters when it comes to improvements. Living in the moment, and paying attention to the people in your lives is paramount to building better relationships. Therefore, it will be important to get the phone numbers and e-mail addresses for all of your distant relatives, and contact them. It will be important to call and see your parents as soon as you can, and to stay present in your children's lives. This will be hard work, but without focus on your family your journey will be less than complete.

Family relationships are the hardest to understand and to potentially improve upon. One very important factor here to stay the course and DO NOT give up. Trust me, I have thought many times about giving up on my family (I'm sure they have had similar feelings), but I have endured, and my family relationships continue to improve.

Before I conclude this all important chapter on family, I would be remiss if I didn't call attention to a critical missing piece to this family equation. The missing piece I am referring to here is that, quite possibly, some of your family relationships are toxic and really not good for your overall health. This is a tough pill to swallow, but it needs to be contemplated and dealt with. You see, this is my back nine and your back nine, NOT the back nine of others in your family. Yes, I personally feel that I can improve on most of my family relationships, but that might not be the case for you. If you have family members that treat you poorly, make fun of you, do not respect you, than it's not likely that your efforts will result in improvements. However, it will be important for you to try and "forgive them" and move on. Don't dwell on these relationships, because the fact is that some people will choose to remain in the "jelly-fish" fields. You will not, which is why you are prepared to work very hard on the family relationships that can and will improve. In the end, it's about the effort that you exert as you set out to make things right. Remember, only you can make those determinations regarding what's best for your life. However, I can guarantee that your hard work will pay off, and your back nine will be filled with more happiness, joy, and fulfillment.

__Back on the course__. Guess what, you have made it through the first hole. You have made a solid par, and you are off to # 11. You hit five excellent shots on this hole, and this will give you confidence for the remainder of your back nine. Remember to "trust your swing," which is another way of saying "trust yourself." You can do this.

#11 – "36 holes in one day" – Par 4

*"I just invented a new acronym for **DIET**:*
D – Don't ever talk about going on a diet again!!
I – Ingest only foods that are good for you. You know what they are!!
E – Exercise every day!!
T – That's it!!"

—Tony Caico

On the course *— #11 is an excruciating par 4, and one of the most difficult holes on the course. You first need to be sure to select the right club off the tee, due to the fact that this hole is very narrow. The fairway is guarded by trees on both sides, and for some reason, the golf course architect decided to place a sand bunker right in the middle of the fairway. Almost unfair, but if you choose the right club on each shot and keep the ball down the middle, the task becomes less daunting. The green is also very small on this hole, and there is water on the left side. This hole could set the stage for the rest of your back nine both positively and negatively. That's OK, you are prepared. Breathe deep, relax, focus, and swing away!!*

Stroke 1 – Health and Wellness

Why is Health and Wellness one of the nine key components? The answer to that question seems obvious, right? Then why do so many of us have such a hard time with this? I will tell you that this has always been a very difficult component for me to tackle. I have struggled with my weight, fitness, and overall health for over fifteen years. As I have stated before, this book has become a proverbial "road map" for my own back nine. Being healthy and fit truly needs to be at the core of everyone's life. We all know that being healthy is so very important, but why is it so difficult? When we make a comparison to golf, one of the key words that jump out at us is "discipline." The great football coach of the Green Bay Packers, Vince Lombardi said it best:

> *"The good Lord gave you a body that can stand almost anything. It's your mind you have to convince. Mental toughness is many things and rather difficult to explain. Its qualities like sacrifice and self-denial. Also, most importantly, it is combined with a perfectly disciplined will that refuses to give in. It's a state of mind-you could call....character in action?"*

I realize that we jumped sports from golf to football, but when it comes to making a point, Lombardi's messages are always crystal clear. To be a good football player or golfer requires a tremendous amount of hard work, dedication, and discipline. Actually, as I stated in the introduction, it is my opinion golf is one of the hardest games to master. It's the self-mastery of golf that makes it so unique as compared to other team sports. When it comes to our all important health and fitness, it is these same qualities (discipline, dedication, focus) that we must draw upon to master this component. To accomplish this feat, we must acquire the necessary knowledge, understand our bodies, exercise regularly, stay on a healthy diet, take vitamins, etc....

We don't really have an option here, folks; health is a critical step to improving our back nine success. As we age, this becomes even more difficult. But remember, this is just our first shot on this hole, so let us first realize the critical nature of this topic. Let us first identify that it needs to be a priority in our lives. If it already is, that's great. Where can you improve? If you need to start from scratch, that's OK. I am somewhere in between, but certainly on the lower end of the scale as far as meeting my objectives. I have gained the knowledge regarding what to eat, which vitamins to take, and what I need to do from an exercise standpoint. My issue has been "executing" the game plan.

Regardless of where you place yourself on this spectrum, understanding that you need a plan and executing that plan are critical components to improving your health. Have you ever heard the phrase "healthy body, healthy mind?" Well, I am here to tell you, once you are able to tackle this component and it becomes part of your life, your confidence level will soar to new heights. Do I know this from experience? No, but I have had glimpses of it before. I have lost a great deal of weight on a few occasions, but it didn't stick because I didn't make it a part of my life. However, I did feel better and more confident as I was losing the weight. I felt better exercising, eating right, and just the journey of staying focused on my health provided me with greater confidence. When you look better, you feel better. Improving our back nine performance will prove difficult if we are not at our best physically. All of the other components, career, relationships, leadership, personal growth, etc., will come easier if we feel better about ourselves and if our health is in check. I am not talking about being perfect and looking perfect here, folks. I am talking about paying attention to your body. What goes in your body, how you treat your body, and how all of this fits into your daily life. That is what *My Back Nine* is all about. What have you done wrong when it comes to your health and fitness, and what can you do to improve?

Back on the course. *Well done!! You made a great club choice on your tee shot here, and your ball is resting squarely in the middle of the fairway. This is easy...right? Well, let's not pat each other on the back just yet; we still have to navigate three more difficult shots on this hole. Remember, the green is very small and there is water on the left. If you are going* *to miss, be sure to miss this shot short and right. Here we go......*

Stroke 2 – Diet

After years of trying many different diets, I have developed and a new and very simple strategy. Eat the right foods at the right time of day, take the right vitamins, eat smaller portions, and stay away from the wrong foods. As far as dieting, I have tried Slimfast, Weight Watchers, Nutrisystem, Subway, and many other diets. All of them work for a short period of time, but the weight always comes back. What I have realized is that for me to be my absolute best, I need to get the weight off and keep it off. That means, stop dieting, and just start eating right. Dr. Oz tells us in his now famous book, *YOU: The Owner's Manual* that we can control our health destiny.

Did you know that you can actually live "ten years younger" than your age from a health perspective? It's true. In order to do this, we need to focus on four very important topics:

- We need to make our health a major priority in our lives (we talked about this in preparation for this chapter)
- We need to gain knowledge about our bodies (we will talk more about this later on this stroke and the next)
- We need to eat the right types of foods, the right portions, at the right times of the day.
- We need to exercise regularly

Seems fairly easy...right? Obviously, we all know that this is not easy. Let's start with diet, and make an attempt to identify with all of the things we put into our bodies during the first half of our lives (our front nine). This includes alcohol, fast food, fried food, ice cream, soda, Krispy Kreme donuts (my personal favorite), and all of the other non-nutritional types of foods we have ingested. For many of us (me included), we never had to worry about this until age thirty or so. That is when the metabolism stats slowing down, you start exercising less, yet you continue to believe you can still consume the same foods. It doesn't take too long to realize what happens to your body after all of that abuse. For me (and many men), the result was a beer belly, which has been a problem I have lived with for over fifteen years. But this is a problem that I am determined to fix, right now, with you. We can do this together. We are changing the way we do things, remember? We are re-setting our compass to head in the right direction. When is comes to food, this requires a tremendous amount of knowledge and discipline, such as saying to yourself, "I will not live with this 'belly' for the rest of my life."

That's my thing. What's yours? What is it about your physical stature that you wish to change? What mistakes have you made that have turned into bad eating habits? For me, it was mostly pasta, steak, starches, fast food, and snacking, accompanied by some heavy drinking. Part of my personal struggle has been exacerbated by my change in marital status. Sounds like another excuse, right? Well, it is, but it's still my reality. Over the last several years I have gained a much greater appreciation of my ex-wife's daily role, as I now have to take care of my kids on my own when I have them. This is an enormous task, especially for someone who has never really taken the time to truly "domesticate." For example, feeding the children is usually accompanied by trips to fast food restaurants in an attempt to avoid cooking and cleaning dishes. This has been a killer for me, not to mention the fact that my kids get very little nutritional value from Happy Meals. This is getting easier for me as time goes on and my children get older. The older boys seem more aware about what they put into their bodies, but we all have a long way to go on this front. Again, this is not about being perfect, but it is about making better decisions on the back nine. Not only for yourself, but for others in your life. Your good habits (or bad) will certainly rub off on the other people in your life, especially your children.

Another killer for me has been creating the time and space for exercise. I was an athlete my entire young adult life, and at about the age thirty or so my activity level started to diminish. Unfortunately, I had already developed the taste for beer, wine, pasta, and steak. I also had an occupation that kept me on the road, traveling and entertaining. How could I take a client out to dinner to a steak restaurant and order fish or chicken? It all boils down to one basic factor on this hole, folks. Self control and self discipline. Many of us need to basically "start from scratch." The first step is to understand our bodies. Remember, learning new things, regardless of your age will be paramount to our back nine success. We are rebuilding here, in some cases (like mine), from the ground up. We need to lay the foundation for the rest of our lives. A healthy body is a great place to begin…don't you think?

As I stated in the introduction (or at the turn), we will use our front nine experiences to examine each of these golf holes (key components), and make the necessary "swing" adjustments to ensure a happier and more fulfilling back nine. For starters, just think of all of the bad things we put into our bodies without recognizing what we were doing to ourselves and how they affect us physically. If you were like me, the last time you learned about how your body actually works you were in junior high school. Do you think it's time for a refresher course? Well, the book I mentioned above, *YOU: The Owner's Manual* is a great place to start. It covers all of our body functions in detail. How things work, what each body part is responsible for, and how they interact with the other body parts. It is an awesome read and will help you gain an intense understanding of your body. It will also help set the wheels in motions to tackle your health and diet concerns. I'm sure there are other great resources for this information, but reading this book is actually fun. They have great diagrams, "myth busting" sections, and practical plans that you can put into play immediately.

After I read it what did I do? Well, for a few months, I made some great progress, but it didn't stick. WHY? Well, I can only figure at this point that I wasn't really ready to make this a priority in my life. Now, that has changed. I have re-read the book, as well as Dr. Oz's other book, *YOU: On a Diet*.

Fortunately, for me, they were staring at me right on my bookshelf, and they are very easy to read. I went through both of them in about a week. Go ahead, "back niners," go out and get those two books right away. You will not be sorry. For example, towards the end of the first book, there is a fantastic crib sheet that identifies the basics of a diet. Keep in mind, the word "diet" here simply means your eating habits…not "going on a diet", which is something that has taken me a long time to learn and was fuel for my "tongue and cheek" quote at the beginning of this golf hole. They cover many simple items, but here are a few:

- Meal schedule – Eat when hungry, not famished, and make your last meal at least three hours before bed.
- Plate size – 9 inches, not the usual 11-13 inch variety.
- Foods to eat daily – 9 handfuls of fruits and vegetables; at least ounce of nuts; whole-grain breads and cereals that contain fiber.
- Food to avoid – Processed foods that contain trans or saturated fats; white foods like creamed sauces, white bread, white rice and simple sugar.; products containing high-fructose corn syrup
- To drink daily – 64 ounces of water, 2 glasses skim or low-fat milk, one glass of red wine.

I recommend these books because of the sheer knowledge you can gain. Once you have the knowledge and are able to grasp a better understanding of the facts, then you are able to make the right food choices. That is what this chapter is all about…having discipline and making better choices, especially when it comes to our diets, and what we put into our bodies. I always liked the car analogy. If you put something into your car that was not the proper combination of oil and gas, your car would absolutely not run. Think about your body the same way. If we educate ourselves about our anatomy, and understand what types of foods to eat, than the game plan becomes easier. We have all taken many unnecessary risks with our bodies during our front nine; I know that is true for me. Let's turn this around together, and treat our bodies right. We will look better, feel better, and live longer, happier lives. That's what the back nine is all about.

Back on the course. Very nice shot. You have landed safely on this small green. You avoided the sand bunker off the tee, and now you have avoided the water in front of the green. Very well done indeed. Your putt is not very long, only about twelve feet. However, behind the hole, the green falls away in a steep fashion. Therefore, pay close attention and do not get too aggressive. You want to have positive thoughts, but you also do not want to make a mistake and end up off the green on the other side of the hole. Good luck.

Stroke 3 – Exercise

We all know that we need to exercise…right? So, again, why is it that we don't? Well, it boils down to focus and discipline. It boils down to finding things we "like" to do. Here's the deal, we absolutely need to find and develop an exercise routine that we will "like, and stick to." Once we do, our lives will immediately improve. All we need to do is take a few small steps, our bodies and minds will be energized, and our back nine will surely improve. Let's start off with something really simple to illustrate my point: What happens to your state of mind when you smile? You automatically feel better, right? Well, there are both emotional and actual physical reasons why smiling is good for us.

I'll get to exercise in a minute, but let's start with this analogy. Take a look at the following facts about smiling and what it does for us:

1. Smiling makes us attractive – Did you ever notice that you are drawn to people who smile. There is an attraction factor. We usually want to know what a smiling person is thinking about, and figure out what is so good. Frowns, scowls and grimaces on the other hand, all push people away. But a smile draws them in.
2. Smiling Changes Our Mood – The next time you are feeling down, try putting on a smile. There's a good chance you mood will change for the better. Smiling can trick the body into helping you change your mood, and the next thing you know you have actually forgotten about what was troubling you in the first place.
3. Try this test: Smile. Now try to think of something negative without losing the smile. It's hard, right? You see, when we smile our body is sending the rest of us a message that "Life is Good!"

26

Now, how cool is that? There are actually many more positive aspects of smiling, but you get the idea. You can be more attractive, successful, positive, and relieve stress just by smiling. Isn't this what the back nine is all about? After I read this, I put a mirror in my office right in front of where I sit to make sure I smile when I'm on the phone. Since I have a home office, it's is easy for me to do. Another idea is to put a mirror in your desk, or even better, a small one next to your computer on your wall. What I have found is that it helps me throughout the day, especially when I have to make many phone calls that day. I know the person on the other end can tell that I'm smiling since it comes through in my voice. Go ahead, try it. The back nine is all about change, making you better. Paying attention to how often we smile can add value to our lives and the lives of the people we connect with. How refreshing.

One of the most interesting concepts in golf is the act of "visualizing your shot." In Darrin Gee's book, *The Seven Principles of Golf*, Visualizing Your Shot is principle #3. Most professional players and many amateurs have a positive visualization of their shot right before they swing. The great Annika Sorenstam says it like this:

"I close my eyes and see the shot. I look at the ball and see the type of shot I have in my mind. I see it fly and then I see it hit land. It's a way of seeing the result before you do it. I visualize the end result."

Well, congratulations folks, that is kind of what we just did by talking about smiling. We used the smile analogy, and the associated positive results to frame our next shot, which is exercise. Now, that we have positive thoughts about the little things our bodies can do, we are ready to get the next step and talk about exercise. In the same light our bodies reacted to very small adjustments like smiling, just imagine how our bodies will react if we extend that effort into a daily workout routine. These routines will vary depending upon your personal goals, but everyone needs to exercise. With the assistance, again, from *YOU, the Owner's Manual*, here are some basic principles that everyone can immediately put into play:

- Thirty minutes of walking every day, no excuses

- Thirty minutes a week of resistance training. Free weights, universal, bow-flex, or any other equipment can be used. Can be broken up into three 10 minute workouts.
- Sixty minutes a week of stamina training. Swimming, cycling, or running. Can be broken up into three 20 minute workouts.
- Thirty minutes of yoga or stretching. Can be broken up into five 5 minute workouts.

Now, I am sure you will agree this is a very minimal workout schedule. However, like many back niners, right now you either are not doing anything or not having a great deal of success at what you are currently doing. So this is a great place to start. There are different methods for stretching, yoga, and strength training in the aforementioned book. Obviously, there are gym memberships, health magazines, and a plethora of other books and programs geared towards helping you exercise and lose weight. My suggestion is to start simple, elevate your base knowledge of exercise, and then find the right plan for you. For example, for me, I love to run. Therefore, I have included running in my routine. However, I also realize that without strength training and stretching, I will not maximize my exercise potential. I have started a program of weight training three times per week, cardio (walking or running) every day, and stretching every day. My plan is to increase my strength training and my stretching (through yoga) as I increase both my strength and my flexibility.

Remember, we are transforming our lives. Even though we all have individual goals to meet, we must stay aware that these workout routines will become a constant part of our daily schedule. Exercising regularly will help us in many other areas of our lives, including:

- *Exercise is good for your heart.*
- *Exercise will help you sleep better at night?*
- *Exercising will release endorphins, which will elevate your attitude and generally put you in a better frame of mind.*
- *Routine exercise will increase your energy level.*

- *Regular exercise also decreases your chance of developing fatigue and exhaustion*
- *Better sex has been linked to higher levels of physical activity.*
- *Exercise, especially morning exercise, can improve your sleep quality.*

I'm not sure about you, but the enormous benefits of exercise really get me excited. Just think, by making this a priority in our lives, we actually realize all of these phenomenal benefits. Don't you think these feelings will be better than the feelings we have after we eat ice cream, chips, or drink all of that beer? You bet...not to mention...no more guilt!!

__Back on the course__. What a great putt. I'm not sure how that putt didn't go in, but it was a perfect stroke. Sometimes the grain of the green, the time of day, or other "unknown" factors creep into play while you're putting. Just like real life...right?? Anyway, nice job. You are only left with a short putt to finish off the hole. Be careful, don't rush the putt. Pay attention to both the line of the putt and the speed. Go ahead, knock it in.

Stroke 4 – Overall healthy living

We have just completed most of the work on this all important hole #11, but let's make sure we don't skip any of the details regarding diet, fitness, and overall healthy living. We have many other parts of our body that need attention. We must take good care of our skin, our teeth, our hair, as well as our other more personal body parts. We must stay focused on our hygiene, our bathing techniques, and pay close attention to the way we look each day. My oldest son has Aspergers Syndrome, which is basically another word for high-functioning autism. He is now a teenager, and is having a hard time with personal hygiene. Although it is frustrating at times, I am enjoying spending time with him focusing on hygiene, and it has helped me dial into things about me I need to improve. For example, he was having difficulty remembering to put deodorant on each day. In order to get his attention, I had to make reference to the nice looking young girls in his class. Being fourteen, he is starting to get interested in girls, although he doesn't really know what to do yet. That's cool, because this gave me the ammunition I needed to keep him focused on how he smells each day. The lesson for me was not far behind. Although I do remember to wear deodorant each day, there are other aspects of my appearance that need to be improved. Specifically, my weight and my dress. You see, I too, have an interest in the opposite sex. In order for me to attract who I am looking for, I need to keep focused in this department, just like my son. If you look at individual people and other goals in your life, it's pretty easy to draw inspiration. You just have to look closer and pay attention.

For me, all of my children provide great inspiration. However, as I witness the struggles of my special needs son, I draw deep inspiration from his courage. He doesn't really understand sometimes what I am trying to say, but he wants to please me, so his listens intently, and enjoys looking at himself in the mirror when we are finished grooming.

All too often, we are not concerned with our appearance. I imagine we all experience this sometimes, but it seems like some people just give up. Well, not for this group of back niners. I am sure you wouldn't be reading this book if you were not concerned about your appearance. After all, this is how you present yourself to the world. I am always leery of the person who says, "I don't care about what other people think!" Do you think there is any way that can be a true (or productive) statement? Of course you should care about what other people think. We are in the process of reshaping and fine-tuning our lives here, folks. We are identifying all of the critical components of our lives and we are working diligently on improvements. Doesn't that include the way we look? Vanity is not always a bad thing. But is it the most important thing? Probably not, but it is definitely an important piece of our overall well being. The way we take care of ourselves and present ourselves in public speaks volumes on how we may conduct ourselves in other parts of our lives. For me, this has been very prevalent over the years. In the past, I have always tried to look my best in business and in social settings. However, when I go out shopping, or to run errands, I have historically not paid attention to the way I look. That is changing for me now. I still wear ball caps and sweatpants, but I make sure my clothes are not wrinkled, my teeth are brushed, my hair is combed, and I look presentable. Now, I pay attention to all of the details, and this has helped me in other aspects of my life. "Paying attention to the details" is very, very important, folks. It's all part of improving our lives, and living better. So, go ahead, put more mirrors around. It will help you with accountability, and build your confidence as you improve each day. Like the guy from the Men's Warehouse says, "I guarantee it."

> ***Back on the course***. *Nice work. Another par. You are progressing along very nicely. That was a very difficult hole, and you played it like a pro. You have set the stage for the rest of your back nine by carefully navigating #11. You could be on your way to your best back nine ever. However, keep your focus on the fundamentals. Pay attention to your grip, your stance, your ball position. Golf is a very funny game, if you lose focus, you could end up in a hazard at any given moment. I sense you will be OK. Now, on to #12.*

#12 – "Do you know your golf game?" – Par 4

"A day without learning is a day without living"

—Lou Holtz

On the course - *#12 is one of the easiest holes on the back nine. I know what you are thinking. "Well, it's about time." Like any golf course, some holes are more challenging than others, but they ALL require the same dedication, preparation, and focus. #12 is a very short par 4, only 325 yards off the tee. It's definitely a birdie opportunity. It's best to play for position off the tee on this hole with either a fairway wood or long iron. The fairway is guarded on both sides by trees, but the landing area is still fairly wide. A solid tee shot will leave you with a very short approach. The green is enormous on this hole, and slopes severely from left to right. The pin position is back right, one of the most accessible places on the green. If you use all of your "wisdom" on this hole, you are sure to have success. It will be helpful to stay mindful of the positive swing thoughts that you have picked up from playing the first few holes. This will help you not only on #12, but throughout your entire back nine. Good luck!*

Stroke 1 - Knowledge

How many times have you heard the phrase "knowledge is power?" If you're like me, you have heard this hundreds of times. What does this really mean? Could it be true? I'm here to tell you that, in my humble opinion, it is absolutely true. Just think about the times you felt super confident. Usually those confident feelings are attached to some sort of knowledge that you have gained about a particular subject or topic, right? Or maybe, it's an occasion that you just look fantastic. But, why do you look fantastic? Yes, you may be blessed with great genes, but you also have gained and retained knowledge about how to stay in shape, how to dress, how to present yourself and look your best. We talked about this in detail on #11. Either way, that confidence typically has a direct correlation to some sort expertise of the subject matter. Listen to what May Sarton says about confidence and how it's gained:

"One does not 'find oneself' by pursuing one's self, but on the contrary by pursuing something else and learning through discipline or routine...who one is and wants to be."

I believe that confidence and knowledge go hand in hand. The fact is that knowledge is something that is gained, over time, and eventually it becomes ingrained in our brains. When we transfer that knowledge into execution, the results can be astonishing. Take a look at this:

Knowledge is defined in the dictionary as: expertise, or skills acquired by a person through experience or education; the theoretical or practical understanding of a subject.

However, the pursuit of this knowledge is something that seems to get put on the back burner at some point in our lives. Typically this happens when we leave some sort of formal education, either high school or college. Our learning mechanisms transition from teachers, text books, and history class; to television, Internet, smart phones, and other forms of media. I'm not saying that we cannot gain insight from television programs and other media outlets; certainly we can from the Internet. My suggestion here is that, at some point and time, our actual pursuit of knowledge shifts. We graduate from high school or college, get a job, and much of our focus and attention goes in that direction. That's perfectly normal. Early in my career, I was in the tire and auto industry, and wanted to learn as much as I could in an attempt to elevate my career. Therefore, most of my focus went into ingesting all I could about cars, tires, and anything else that would provide me with a competitive edge. I remember learning about tire tread wear ratings, water disbursement, brake pads and rotors, wheel alignments, shock absorbers, and anything else that would help me communicate with and educate the consumer. After that, I moved into financial services, specifically the mortgage banking business (more of that in the career section). So, naturally, my focus shifted to learning about that industry. Interest rates, loan programs, underwriting guidelines, appraisals, and other items that would, again, help me educate my customer. I was pretty much "single-focused" on the topics that I needed to know to perform my job function at a high level. Again, this was perfectly natural and very typical of our learning focus when we choose a certain career path.

To be honest, I never really enjoyed reading until I started my business career. Like many young male adults, my reading was relegated to the sports page and an occasional magazine. Usually, a sports magazine. Actually, when I took up golf in my mid-twenties, I picked up every golf magazine I could get my hands on to learn about the game, what clubs to use, what courses to play, and what the professionals were doing. As soon as I moved into sales management, I started to read more avidly, but mostly business books about sales, coaching, and leadership. Like I said, all of this was perfectly natural, and I never realized what I was missing. Sort of like "you don't know what you don't know." A few years back, what I started to realize is that I totally left out so many important and interesting topics. Like many others, I lost focus on my *pursuit of knowledge*. Somewhere along the line, I stopped investing in the incredible power of my brain. We are all born with fantastic brains capable of achieving greatness. According to most scientists, we only use about 10% (or less) of our brain capacity. Now that we are on our back nine journey, maybe it's time to start soaking up more information. There are so many incredible things to learn, and quite frankly, most of us stopped investing in our brain capacity years ago.

I have learned so much in the last few years, and now I can't get enough. I am constantly reading. Every day, I read from a book entitled *The Intellectual Devotional*. It is 365 pages of daily subject matter in the areas of science, history, music, philosophy, arts and literature, and religion. It's an incredible book, and I just found out that there is a new version. The main point here is that there are so many interesting things to learn, and that this focus on learning could just become the key for us back niners to ignite the fire within. The fire that has always been there, we just let it go for a while. You see… *knowledge is power.*

A few weeks ago, I was reading about Benjamin Franklin in another book I read from often. It has the ultimate "TMI" (too much information) book title, *Passing Time in the Loo.* What an amazing person this man was. Among other things, he was an accomplished writer, a prominent businessman, a respected political figure, an inventor, and a librarian. A true Renaissance Man. I can tell you, that reading about this Mr. Franklin really put the wind in my sails. What I have learned about myself in recent years is that there is virtually no subject that I am not interested in. I truly enjoy sports, music, business, politics, religion, relationships, self awareness, science, history, philosophy, pop culture, psychology, as well as many other topics.

For me, gaining knowledge on these topics now seems so natural, but it wasn't always like that. Like many folks on the front nine, I was only focused on items that directly affected my life at the time. That's OK. Remember what we talked about in the introduction (the turn) of this book. It generally takes time, experiences, and a deep understanding of who we are before we are actually ready to tap into the 90% of our unused brain capacity. Knowledge and education are critical components of our back nine, folks. Our quest is to learn flows in concert with our quest to improve. Just look at the first two holes (family and health). Didn't we first have to gain the knowledge about these topics in order to set the course for improvement? This premise will be identical for every single golf hole on this back nine. The good news is that, once we get the wheels in motion and change our way of thinking, the rest will come easy. Really, it will. We just need to stay focused on carving out time to learn. Just like on the last hole on diet and fitness, it all boils down to discipline.

But first, we must realize that this self-discovery we gain by learning is important in our lives, and make a decision to keep focused on it daily. As you pave your way though these golf holes, you will find that some topics will resonate more soundly with you than others. That's perfectly OK. I am attempting to help you by using my experiences and my goals for the future to frame these items out for you. This is truly *My Back Nine*. However, my hope is that you will develop your own back nine strategies. Knowledge will be a constant as you unpack each component of your back nine.

> *Back on the course. Nice tee shot, again. 220 yards, right down the middle. Nice club choice. You have left yourself with a very manageable short iron into this large green. Remember, the green slopes from right to left. Therefore, you don't want to miss right. You are ready for this shot, now dial in and strike!!*

Stroke 2 – Process - How do I obtain and retain knowledge?

Well, I think the first step here is something that we already accomplished on our first stroke on this hole. That is, we have identified that learning needs to be a priority in our lives. Making this leap may be harder for some than others, but in my view, the rewards are endless. Just paying attention to the fact that we must continue to tap into our brain power will provide us with greater capacity not only to learn, but to actually retain that knowledge. We will talk more about what we will do with this knowledge on our next stroke, but let's stay focused by acknowledging that we need to constantly feed our brains. What you will begin to learn is that you have way more capacity than you might think. Not only will you realize that you can ingest more, but the more you ingest the easier it actually is to retain that knowledge. It's sort of like feeding our bodies with the vitamins and nutrients we spoke about on #11. The brain works the same way. It actually has the power to control everything in your body. However, as we age, our brain needs extra work to keep it functioning like it did when we were younger.

Learning and physical fitness actually increase brain power. Let me say this again, our brains will lose capacity while we age if we don't do anything about it. However, studies have shown that your actual IQ can increase over time if you stay engaged, stay fit, and keep active…both mentally and physically. If you don't work your muscles, they will turn into flab. The brain works the same way. Either use it or lose it, so to speak. You need to stay dialed in on stretching yourself mentally each day. The best way to do this is to learn something new, everyday. Which is why I read from my *Intellectual Devotional* (I love the way that sounds) everyday. The more you learn, the more you stretch your brain's capacity. Another way to increase your brain function is to daydream. Yes, that's right *daydream*.

Using your imagination takes your brain out of its normal functions and stimulates a different section of the brain. It may help to gather up a few daydreaming topics and store them in your memory bank. For instance, what is your "perfect day?"

For me, it goes something like this:

"I awake in my beachfront home to the sounds of the ocean. I get up, have a nourishing and delicious breakfast with eggs (over-medium), cheese grits, fresh tomatoes, Rye toast, fresh-squeezed orange juice, accompanied up by a fabulous fresh cup of coffee. All of this while sitting on my deck, over-looking the golf course and the ocean. I take a long, hot shower in my "duel-headed", "high-powered" shower stall. I put my golf clothes on, and go to the garage to get in my personalized golf cart. I take the short ride to the ocean golf course, and waiting for me at the clubhouse are three of my children, my ultimate foursome, for sure. We play a fabulous round of golf together, and then gather back at the house for a cookout. You see, it's Superbowl Sunday, and the New York Giants are playing…again. But before the game starts, I head back over to the health club for a full body massage. Nice. Another shower, and I head back to the house.

We all watch the Giants win, enjoy each other's company, and eat some great food (possibly a pasta dish, some fresh seafood, and an assortment of awesome football food). After the kids leave, I sit down to relax with my incredible significant other (she's not here yet, but I am daydreaming— remember!!), a nice Pinot Noir, and some soft music."

Just writing that piece felt really good. Now I know that whenever I go there, my brain actually increases its capacity. Now, that is news you can use, my friends. Isn't this what the back nine is all about?

Also, changing your routine is helpful. One thing we will learn throughout this back nine is that we need to develop routines, strategies, and game plans to improve our lives. However, changing those routines from time to time will actually increase your brain functionality. As long as you get it all in, it's OK to change things up a bit. Go ahead, try all of these things. You'll be glad you did.

Another fantastic way to continue to gain knowledge is to read everyday. To improve your learning capacity, I would recommend that you read a variety of different types of books, magazines, newspapers, etc. I started this a few years ago, and I haven't stopped. Like I mentioned before, I have a renewed quest for learning. I would even suggest that you read from a few different books during the same time period. Remember, the health of your brain increases with its use. Right now, I am reading three books at the same time, all with different subject matter. *Uncommon* (Tony Dungy), *Golf is not a Game of Perfect* (Bob Rotella), and *The Bible* (too many to mention)!!

Lastly, trying new things that you haven't experienced before is an excellent way to increase your knowledge and brain function. The brain seems to like discomfort. Whether it's sky diving (not for me), cooking classes (I love these), or ballroom dancing (would do it, but haven't yet) trying new activities is both exhilarating and rewarding. How often have you told yourself: "I would really like to learn a new language?" Well, what is stopping you? This is the back nine of our lives, folks, and this is the time where we actually do the things we have always wanted to do. Most of us have gained the knowledge regarding the things we no longer should do, but have we truly thought about the things that we have always wanted to do?

Last year, I saw the movie *The Bucket List* with Jack Nicholson and Morgan Freeman. Both of the characters are dying and while they are in the hospital they come up with a list of things they have always wanted to do. It's a great movie and the acting is, of course, incredible. It really got me thinking about living now, and not waiting or worrying about what will happen in the future. Sure, you can't do everything now, but making a list is a great place to start. I never was one for writing things down, but that has changed for me. Now, I write everything down and log my thoughts into one of my electronic files.

Another great example of making lists comes from another book that I read last year entitled, *Wins, Losses, and Lessons*, by the great football coach, Lou Holtz. As a matter of fact, I received an autographed copy from Lou himself after he spoke at a national sales conference I attended with my former employer. I was a special moment in my life. Early in his coaching career, Lou sat down and made a list of 108 things that he wished to accomplish. I realize that this is an extreme example of list making, but it has resonated with me ever since I read it, and I hope you can draw inspiration from what he did as well. He broke the list down into five categories, with the last being "things I always wanted to do." A few items on the list were: "jump out of an airplane," "appear on *The Tonight Show*," "go on a submarine,", "have dinner at The White House" and "meet the Pope." He actually made this list before he had achieved any great success as a coach. The amazing thing about this story is that, at the time of his book publishing, Lou Holtz had achieved all but two items on his original list. How's that for achieving your goals?

Obviously, you don't need 108 items, nor do you want to wait until you are facing death to do all of things you have always wanted to do. You can start now. Go ahead, stop reading, pull out a pen and paper and make your list. Start with just ten items. I'll tell you what; I will do the same thing, right now. I'll be back in a minute and tell you mine.

OK, here is my top ten (in no particular order):

1. Go to Italy

2. Take my children to Washington, DC
3. Write a book (☺)
4. Own my own business
5. Go to the US Open
6. Go to the Final Four
7. Go to Napa Valley on a wine tour
8. Play Pebble Beach
9. Play St. Andrews
10. Go to Hawaii

That was really cool. I just felt the same rush I had when I wrote down what my "perfect day" looked like. Did you feel it? If not, you may want to re-visit your list. We are taking a serious journey into our minds on this back nine. We are digging deep to find our "authentic self". We are obtaining and retaining knowledge by reading, learning (and doing) new things and exercising our brains, every day.

Back on the course. That was an awesome wedge shot, my friend. You landed the ball in the perfect position in the middle of the green, with a nice cut, and it has nestled up only about six feet from the pin. You are poised for your birdie. Take your time, as this putt has about a two- foot break from right to left. It's a bit uphill, so you can hit it firm. Exactly where you want to be. All you need to do is execute.

Stroke 3 – Practice - What do I do with all of this knowledge?

The last shot on this hole is quite easy in light of the fact that your first two shots on this hole were so perfect. We have now have a firm understanding of why learning and gaining knowledge is so very important in our lives. We also have some new tips and tricks on how to obtain (and retain) all of this important subject matter. Now, all we have to do is execute this very short putt and put our knowledge into play.

Here's the easy part. The knowledge that you gain will be used to fulfill your objectives on ALL of other eight components on your back nine. You now know how your brain works and what you need to do to build your brain capacity. You have armed yourself with some reliable and useful tools to ingest and digest this knowledge. All of this information will help you navigate your entire back nine with great success. Let's take one hole at a time, starting with the two holes we have already played.

This exercise will be both a recap of the first two holes, as well as a prelude to the next five:

Family (#10) – We looked back at our childhood to see what we learned both positively and negatively. We looked at our individual family relationships, and thought about what we want to do to improve each one of them. We looked at our conditioned behaviors, and potentially made some in-roads to where we made good choices as well as where we may have steered off course. This self-evaluation certainly has triggered something inside us, and now we must develop a game plan to improve. By looking back and inside, we may have regained some insight into what we need to do better in the second half of our lives in terms of our family, our family relationships, and our own self improvement.

Health and Fitness (#11) – We got a refresher course in the importance of health and fitness in our lives. We came to the realization that we should probably stop "dieting" and should just eat healthy foods that nourish our bodies. We learned that daily exercise is paramount to our overall lives, and that we should keep a daily log of our workouts and food intake.

Knowledge (#12) - We are here now, learning about learning!

Career (#13) – We will look back and examine the components that lead to our career choices. We will then translate those ideas and activities into what we are doing today. We will take a close look at our strengths, weaknesses, and how they correlate to our career path. Lastly, we will use the knowledge of our past, present, and future key indicators to guide us towards our ultimate career aspirations.

Spirituality (#14) – This will be a long but extremely rewarding par 5. We will delve into our soul to try and find meaning in our lives. We will attempt to understand different points of views, religions, and other forms of spirituality. We will use this knowledge to help us find our true path, our ultimate "purpose" in life. This will be fun!!

Leadership (#15) – We will learn that, regardless of one's chosen field of endeavor, that everyone is a leader. We will look at leadership qualities, strategies, and identify for each other where we can make improvements in our lives through leadership.

Relationships (#16) – We will learn why relationships are so important in everything we do. We will analyze our past, present, and potential future relationships and learn to make the necessary adjustments to ensure improvements. We will attempt to understand the importance of how we impact others, and what that means to both our lives and their lives. Who we "partner" with on this hole will determine a great deal on how successful our back nine will be!

Personal Growth/Self Improvement (#17) – This will be a crucial point in our journey. We will learn what it means to actually improve and what that looks like. We will analyze our journey up until #17, and try and draw a connection to the last hole, Happiness.

Happiness (Peace/Enlightenment) (#18) – There are so many individual components that determine our happiness, but we will have covered all of the important topics on holes ten through seventeen.

We conclude here because this is our ultimate goal…to achieve peace and happiness. This last hole will be worth the wait, and all of our hard work will pay off, you'll see. Knowledge and learning lies at the core of everything we aim to achieve on our back nine round of golf on this incredible journey. I hope you are enjoying yourselves as much as I am. My grip feels good, my muscle memory is intact, and I'm ready for # 13, are you?

__Back on the course__. Nice putt…your first "birdie", sweet! There is an old golf saying that "you drive for show…but you putt for dough." Meaning your putting can be either your savoir or your downfall. This was a short, but tricky putt, and you pulled it off admirably. This putting stroke will certainly come in handy as we head into the midway point of our back nine. You are doing awesome so far. Keep it up!

#13 – "Course Management?" – Par 4 -

"Be careful not to build an unbreakable bond between what you do for a living and who you are as a person. All that matters is the latter. However, one who endeavors to build this bond in reverse order opens the door to limitless possibilities"

— Tony Caico

On the course - *Not surprising to you, I am sure, #13 is definitely not as manageable or easy to navigate as #12. As a matter of fact, it's probably one of the more difficult holes on the back nine. There is water directly in front of you off the tee that extends about 210 yards. Therefore, your tee shot needs to clear at least 225 yards to be safe from the hazard. It's quite a challenge to start this hole. After a solid drive, you are faced with more obstacles. The water hazard continues down the left side, and the right side of the fairway is guarded by two enormous waste bunkers (which means there is usually vegetation growing and you can ground your club). To add to the difficulty, the green is surrounded by sand in the front and on the left side. Your second shot will need to be very accurate to hit this small green. If indeed you are fortunate enough to land on the green, the pin placement is right up from, only about 20 feet in front of the sand bunker. Please bear in mind that the 13th hole is a very important part* *of your back nine, as you will spend much time in thought on each shot. In addition, it's typical for the wind to be directly in your face on #13, making the task even more daunting. This challenge will require you to stay calm, focused, and centered as you carefully prepare for each stroke. Are you scared? I didn't think so.*

Stroke 1 - Career

Let's start this grueling golf hole with a close look at the basic time element of this component. On average, most people work about eight hours per day or about forty hours per week. If we take a few weeks' vacation per year, we end up working about two thousand hours per year. If we work fifty years (which is typical these days), we will spend about a hundred thousand hours working throughout our lifetime. Let's just say we live until the ripe old age of ninety (my personal minimum goal for life expectancy). If we deduct the hours for sleeping (let's assume eight hours per day), we will have lived approximately five hundred thousand hours. So, basically, we will spend a fifth of our entire lives (awake, that is) at work. Let's now imagine that we didn't start working until we were twenty, and we are fortunate enough to retire when we are seventy (which is more realistic than sixty five these days). If we deduct the two hundred and thirty hours that lie outside our "career zone," the actual working hour calculation looks a bit more daunting. Now, instead of spending a fifth of our waking hours working, the more realistic number is thirty seven percent. More than a third of our lives will be spent working in some fashion, from the time we reach twenty until the time we reach seventy. Just based on these facts, surely we can ascertain why the career component of our back nine in so important.

Now you know just one of reasons why that this will be such a difficult hole to navigate. It takes a really long time to play this golf hole. You see, what we do "for a living" or "to earn income" is a grueling, yet vital part of our lives and even more crucial during our back nine years. Now, more than ever, our ability to earn is being tested. Many of us, including me these days, are quite often looking into alternative sources of income. For example, as I sit here today, I do have a fairly good job. Not near as good as my former job, both in the type of work and compensation, but I am very thankful to be employed when so many of my colleagues are still unemployed. Like I mentioned earlier, I was in mortgage banking, and that industry has been turned upside down in recent years. More on that later, down the fairway a bit. Based on the facts above, I am considering starting a new business, and always look at opportunities when they come across my desk. The job market is very unstable these days, so the term "career" really takes on a whole new meaning in the current economy. I was actually considering changing the name of this life component, but when I started doing the math and realized the amount of actual time we spend working, I felt even stronger that we need to stay focused and call it what it is, *a career.* I was aided in this decision by Webster's definition:

Career - "Profession, specialty, field (business); course of life, orbit, pilgrimage (life)"

Our course of life, our pilgrimage, what a perfect description to assist us as we play this golf hole together. As I mentioned above, this pilgrimage occupies over one third of our lives, and taking a Polaroid, right now, is a perfect way to dissect this component. It's also very prevalent in light of the stark reality many of us are faced with in these tough economic times. Many of us are going through some really hard financial and emotional times right now, and sometimes we just forget who we are, and what we are here to do, because what we used to do is no longer a part of our lives. For me, the height of my depression was centered on the fact that I was no longer a leader of hundreds of salespeople. I was just a leader of one person, me. But in the end, what I have realized is that what happened in the past doesn't matter, and should only be used as a frame of reference.

All that matters is what we do now. In the end (or beginning), we are to find ourselves again, regardless of the pain, suffering, and/or hardships we go through. It's not about winning, it is not about losing, it's about living! The old quote that *"life is a journey not a destination"* is one of the most important, relevant, and flat out spot-on quotes of all time. Something to live by, for sure. Remember, we ALL have a choice. What will you choose? Will you choose to wallow in self pity and keep thinking about the past? Trust me, I have tried that and it doesn't work. Or will you choose to grab hold of your life, make the necessary "swing changes" and start hitting the ball back down the middle with determination and clarity. My guess is the latter, which is why you are here. Here with me, discovering together what needs to be done to create this incredible back nine we are about to have. Since we spend so much time in this career section of our lives, we must keep our eye on the target at all times. What's the target? Well, it is different for everyone, but ultimately, it's finding our true "career path" after we get our "swing back." You see, all of these life components will end up fitting together for us and will help us spin the spider web that will enable up to capture our back nine dreams and goals. This is what *My Back Nine* is about, my friends. Putting all of these fantastic pieces together, that ultimately makes up the tapestry of our lives.

It's all about finding our one, true authentic self. Clearing the baggage from our past, opening up our minds and our hearts, and creating a powerful new life that flows in perfect harmony with who we were always meant to be. In order to achieve this we must first let go of the past, stop connecting to our circumstances, and move forward. This reminds me of one of my favorite pieces of dialog from the incredible movie, *The Legend of Bagger Vance*:

Bagger Vance*: I don't need to understand... Ain't a soul on this entire earth ain't got a burden to carry he don't understand, you ain't alone in that... But you been carryin' this one long enough... Time to go on... lay it down...*

Rannulph Junah*: I don't know how...*

Bagger Vance*: You got a choice... You can stop... Or you can start...* Clearly, our careers represent an enormous part of who we become. However, it's very important that we keep this in perspective. Many of us (certainly this is true of me) let our careers take hold of our lives. We end up thinking that our "worth" is about what we do, what we can acquire, and what we have. When the reality is that what we do and what we have has no correlation to who we are. This is a lesson that I have learned the hard way, but one that I thank God for every day. My life is different now. It has more meaning, because I realize that I am in control, that I am truly the captain of my own ship. I still have a long way to go, but I am starting to feel really good. How about you?

> ***Back on the course***. *Very nice start to this hole. Your tee shot cleared the water hazard, and you are positioned well on the left side of the fairway. You are really starting to get the hang of this, and I am personally very proud of each and every one of you. Remember, I am your playing partner on this back nine, and we are playing these golf holes together. We still have water down the left side, so pick a spot on the right side of the green as your target. We will be going back into the deep caverns of our minds on this next shot, so our muscle memory will certainly come in handy. Let's remember together!*

Stroke 2 – What did you want to be when you grew up?

What were your dreams and goals, and what is the comparison to your career now?

I will warn you right up front here, my friends, this stroke will be challenging. As we have discussed, in order to clear the path and help create the back nine of our dreams, it will be necessary to go back and identify with our thoughts from the past. We have already done that on numerous occasions in this book, and we will continue this exercise until we are through. Some parts of our past will be more difficult than others, but it's critical that we dissect our thoughts in order to undercover or discover our true path. With regard to our careers, what many of us will find is that the career path we ended up in has absolutely no connection to our initial thoughts and dreams of what life was going to be like. That's perfectly OK, my friends, and very common. The task here will be to guide ourselves towards making some harsh and potentially radical decisions about where we go from here. We may find that we have had great careers, made lots of money, but somehow lost ourselves along the way. That's definitely what happened to me. Again, this is not time to beat ourselves up (trust me, I've tried that as well), it is time for us to evaluate our current career position and decide what we are going to change…if anything. Some of us may not require many changes at all, but I'm guessing that most of us will need to make some alterations.

In true *My Back Nine* fashion, let me frame this out for you by telling my "career" story….from the beginning to present day. Another warning, you should buckle up for this one. We will cover every inch of the thirtieth hole with this tale. We will play from the woods, hit the ball in the water, go out of bounds a few times, and confront almost every hazard on the course (not literally, of course). The moral of this piece will be very important to the overall theme of this golf hole and this journey.

When I was a child, most of my dreams were centered on sports. Yes, I know, you are not surprised. I absolutely adored all sports, and still do. Playing sports was the highlight of my day from the time I was five or six right up until the end of my college days. Of course, I still have days where golf is my highlight, especially on my yearly golf trips with friends. Great times, indeed. The first dream I can remember when I was a young boy was that I wanted to be a professional basketball player. I was a gifted athlete in many sports, but basketball was my first love. As a matter of fact, basketball was my favorite sport until I discovered golf in my early twenties. Now, basketball takes a back seat to golf. If it didn't, this book may have been entitled, *The Second Half.* I remember playing basketball almost every day in my early years. It didn't matter if it was basketball season or not, I still played every chance I could. I was so into basketball that I knew every single NBA player on every team. I used to play imaginary games on the court on the side of my house, and would play the role of all ten players. I would actually pass the ball to myself, play the entire, game, track team standings, and keep the stats for each player. This used to dive my older brother insane and caused a great deal of controversy in the back yard. You see, he would come out and want to play, but I wouldn't let him because I was in the middle of my imaginary game. He would go crazy, but I wouldn't give in until I was finished. I drove him crazier because it was really the only sport that I could compete with him in, and actually could even beat him from time to time. That was a big deal and confidence builder for me, because my brother was also a fine athlete, and even better than me in most sports. But in basketball, I could hold my own against him, and most of the neighborhood kids, but only after I was done with my "imaginary" game. I remember thinking how cool it would be to be Walt Frazier, or Earl (the Pearl) Monroe. They were both guards, like me, and both had a genuine sense of "flair" off the court. Something that also appealed to my senses.

I also idolized Dave Debusher, Bill Bradley, and Willis Reed (the other three players that made up the starting five) for their intelligence and team play. Yes, I was a New York Knicks fan, but the Knicks were actually an awesome team when I was a kid. I know, it's hard to believe now, but they actually won two NBA championships in 1970 and 1973, and they are still my favorite professional basketball team. But, my all-time favorite hoops player at the time was the man himself, Dr. J (Julius Erving). He was my idol, and wore the number that would stay with me forever, **#32** (more on the significance of that number later). Anyway, as I grew older and started to play more competitively, I realized that my dream of becoming a professional was clearly out of reach. I was better than most where I lived, but I couldn't really compete with the New York City kids. Reality sunk in, and I remember it was a very unsettling feeling. Over time, I let it go, and soon set my sights on becoming a gym teacher and coach. I could still be around sports, and I already had a knack for coaching the other players on the team. In addition, I became very good friends with the athletic director of my high school, and to me, he had the coolest job in the world. He really took a genuine interest in his students and I was impressed with the way he connected with people and helped them through some difficult situations, especially me.

The key points that I will come back to later on this important golf hole are: *Coaching, connecting with people, and a genuine interest in helping others.*

After high school, I was fortunate enough to land an athletic scholarship to play soccer at a local college. My parents were thrilled, and I was on my way to a higher education. I remember that it was a little bittersweet, though, because I really wanted to play basketball in college. Unfortunately, I was just not good enough (or tall enough) to get the attention of colleges. I never really liked soccer as much as basketball, but the competition for that sport wasn't as great where I lived, so I became an all-county soccer player my senior year in high school. Anyway, I felt proud to get an athletic scholarship, and I figured I could go to school, graduate, then go back and be a gym teacher as well as a successful basketball coach. To this day, if someone asks me if I could be anything what it would be, I always say a college basketball coach. Of course, a professional golfer would be just as cool, but I digress. After a few months in college, I realized that there just wasn't going to be enough money in being a gym teacher, so I let that go as well, and set my sights on a business career, although I had nothing specific in mind.

I just thought that I would figure that out later. I was living the "college life" and having way too much fun to focus on the future. After college, I started to look for jobs, mostly in the sports marketing and sales industry. I remember applying for quite a few jobs and finally got an interview with Titleist (golf balls). I was never actually offered the job, but the starting salary was eighteen thousand dollars. At the time, I was a bartender, and I was making much more money than eighteen thousand. I was also having a ton of fun, living in Florida, going to the beach, and playing golf quite often. Who wanted to give all that up to sell golf balls? I was swayed by greed and money and unfortunately started picking up many of my bad habits while working as a bartender. Not surprising, I know. I bartended for about three more years, but it started to wear on me after a while. I started thinking that in order to get serious about my life I had to get a real job, a career. I had a college degree, some good communication skills, and I knew I should be doing something else with my life.

A friend of mine had a brother-in-law that was in the tire and auto business. He worked for an up and coming retail tire chain, and offered me a position as a tire salesman. I was reluctant at first, because I really didn't have much interest in cars and tires. I was sports guy, a restaurant guy, a "player," not a tire guy! I was surprised when he told me how much money I could make, and he told me that I could excel in this industry and at his company. So, I decided to take the plunge into the tire business. Well, it turned out to be a really good decision for me, and set the wheels in motion for what would become an exciting business career. For some reason, selling tires and auto services came really easy to me. From my first day, I felt very comfortable talking to customers, learning about tires, and was very eager to start a career. I had always had a strong work ethic, and it was definitely needed for this business. I always tell people that "I cut my teeth" in the retail tire and auto business, and I truly enjoyed my time in that business. I had a boss who was very tough, but also very polished and knowledgeable. He was a bit of a dictator, but got away with it due to his personality and in depth knowledge of the company and the business. I learned a lot from him, and I am grateful for the things he taught me. Our business relationship ended badly, but years later he told me, "Tony, you we one of the best I had ever seen, a natural." Anyway, I elevated rapidly through this company. Within my first three months I became an assistant manager. Within one year, I was a store manager. A year later I was a district manager, and that same year was promoted to regional vice president over forty five retail tire stores on the west coast of Florida.

In three short years, I was managing over four hundred people. It was an exciting time, and I am quite sure that we "revolutionized" the tire industry in Florida during that five year span. We started hiring educated young professionals to work in our tire stores, and created a new and fresh atmosphere for people buying tires and auto services. As many of you know, this isn't the most exciting and pleasurable buying experience, but we made it better and more comfortable for our consumers which lead to increased revenue for the company.

As with most endeavors, the most important aspect of success resides in your ability to bring on the best people. The company experienced incredible growth and we had built a strong and reliable team throughout the state. That was an awesome experience, and I have used the experience I gained in this industry in everything I have done since in my career. I wouldn't change a thing about that time. It was great. After about seven years in the tire and auto industry I started to get the "itch" to do something else. I wasn't sure what to do, so I started looking into owning my own company. I looked into buying a used car lot, but soon realized that it wasn't really a good idea. Then, something really amazing happened. I got a call from a friend of mine who was a loan officer for a mortgage company. They were in the middle of what he called a "refi boom" and he told me that I could make some serious money in the mortgage business. You guys see where this is going, right?

I left my secure position in the tire industry to work a "commission only" job as a loan officer. Well, here's where the story gets really good. After a few months working as a loan officer, I received a call from a friend of mine in Florida. He found out through another friend that I was in the mortgage business. It just so happens, that he was having dinner that evening with the new East Coast president of lending for a large up and coming mortgage banking company. He said that he wanted me to talk with this person, so we spent about thirty minutes on the phone talking about my employment history and his new company. Towards the end of the conversation he asked me if I would be interested in joining his company as an account executive. I said, "What does an account executive do?" He replied, "Well, we actually lend the money to the company that you are working for now as a loan officer." That sounded really good to me. So, the next day, I received a faxed job offer to work for this new mortgage bank based in California, and I would be only the seventh salesperson on the entire East Coast with no territory boundaries. I just got promoted in the mortgage business, and I didn't even do anything yet. The job was accompanied by a salary, an expense account, and a corporate American Express card, not to mention three weeks in Pasadena, for training. Wait, it gets better. After about six months working as an account executive in a new and exciting industry, the company that I worked for rolled out a revolutionary product. They invented a new and proprietary automated underwriting system for alternative lending (which means non-conventional). It was the first of its kind, and there was very little competition for this advanced technology. My loan production doubled in three months, and I was starting to make more money that I ever dreamed possible. I knew we had something special, so I set out to learn as much as I could about the way the system worked. I was fortunate enough to meet one the IT folks that was very close to the inventor of this system, and he educated me on all of the intricacies of the model, including the details of how it evaluated risk to price and approve loans. I became very familiar with the system and started to present this system to mortgage brokers up and down the east coast. This was my first real experience with public speaking to large groups of people, a part of the job that I truly enjoyed. We did about six seminars over a period of three to four months, and the loan production exploded. It was during that time that I was fortunate enough to meet one of the true mentors (I only had two) of my career, who became the new president of lending on the East Coast. You see, I had extensive management experience before, and with the company growing the way it was, this person was looking for a new sales manager. I played in instrumental role with the automated underwriting system and presentations, and got the attention of some key executives throughout the organization. So, after about one year as an account executive, I was promoted into a management position.

I really enjoyed my time at this company, as they were very unique in the mortgage industry. For me, it was a perfect fit, mostly because I wasn't tainted by any other mortgage company, and I thought everything we did made sense. I ended up staying at that company for about seven years, and was very fortunate to have had three separate management positions during my tenure. It was a very exciting time for me, and my career was exploding. I found myself in a new industry, yet I was basically doing the same job I did in the tire and auto industry. I was managing sales people, and I loved my job. As my career grew, there were many other companies venturing into the mortgage wholesale space. I was recruited by a few more companies to help them start up their endeavors over the next five years, and parlayed my experiences to get a better position at each bank. My last wholesale mortgage position was the best of all. I ended up working for the largest bank in the world, and that was just incredible. I started off as a regional sales manager, and two years later I was divisional vice president for the entire eastern half of the U.S. In 2006, my sales group produced over $6 billion in mortgage loans. I traveled extensively, went to conferences, worked from my home office, and had the absolute best job in the world.

My mortgage career took me to over forty states in the US, and I have been fortunate to visit most of the great cities across the country. New York, Chicago, LA, Las Vegas, Dallas, Boston, Atlanta, Miami, Phoenix, Tampa, Detroit, Columbus, Columbia, Charlotte,

Orlando, Cleveland, Denver, San Diego, St. Louis, New Orleans, D.C., Baltimore, Portland, and Seattle. I'm sure I missed a few, but you get the point. I was truly blessed and overall, very proud of my accomplishments. I was making huge money, and thought it would last forever. Well, if you read my introduction, you know how that story ends, or begins, depending on your perspective. For me, it's a beginning. A beginning of a back nine journey that I can't wait to create. I am hopeful that you are feeling the same way. I feel honored to take this journey with you. We are learning about ourselves, and the empowerment that accompanies self-evaluation will help us in everything we do from here on out.

Now, let's bring this back to center. Again, I hope that while you read my version of my career path, you were thinking about your own. The jobs, the places, the people, and the experiences you have had, both good and bad. As I look back upon the things I wanted early in life, I breathe a bit easier knowing that I have actually stayed closer than I thought I did to my initial dreams and goals. I didn't make it to be a professional basketball player, and I have never been a gym teacher of basketball coach. (Well, that's not entirely true. I did coach my six-year olds basketball team this past year, and we went undefeated!). However, I did spend time helping people, I did spend time coaching people, and I have connected with thousands.

Do you remember we spoke about finding our true selves? Sometimes it's about "remembering" our true selves. The good news here is that "you are who you are," and all you have to do is clear the path and "remember." After all I have been through over the last two years; I am starting to realize that I am living the life that I was meant to live. All of my past mistakes, poor decisions, and trials have lead me to this moment. Let me tell you that it "feels fantastic," and gives me a real sense of freedom that I have never had before. I now have the ability to understand that this is where I was meant to be, at this moment in time. How about you, can you see that? This is the path…but where we go from here has everything to do with what we now know about ourselves. My story above is so vivid for me, it's like it all just happened. My awareness has elevated. Can you guys feel that starting to happen? I hope so. For me, I can now "watch myself" from outside as I make decisions and perform tasks. I live more consciously and authentically with this new understanding.

In his incredible book, *The Power of Now*, Eckhart Tolle describes this phenomenon at "being present" or "watching the thinker." Mr. Tolle goes on to say:

"The beginning of freedom in the realization that you are not "the thinker". The moment you start watching the thinker, a higher level of consciousness becomes activated. You then begin to realize that there is a vast realm of intelligence beyond thought, that thought is only a tiny aspect of that intelligence. You also realize that all the things that truly matter.....beauty, love, creativity, joy, inner peace......rise from beyond the mind. You begin to awaken."

Back on the course*. Now, that was a tough shot. So tough, that you went a little off course, and your golf ball has "plugged" in the sand bunker left of the green. Don't worry; you are still in good position, since the pin is on the other side of the green. You can execute this shot with determination and courage. Two items that have followed you on the course all day. Since your ball is "plugged," you will need to keep the clubface open and you need to hit straight down at the ball...so you can get the ball up and over the lip of the bunker. You have performed this shot before; you just have to "remember." Fortunately, you just learned how to "remember"...so you should be good to go.*

Stroke 3 – What are your strengths?
Your weaknesses?

How do they mesh with your career path to date?

If you are anything like me, your career path has taken you in many different directions. What I have found very interesting about this, is that the factors that control this path are usually factors that end up lying beyond our control. Quite often, we make career decisions based on what others are doing, what family members think, the financial implications, and geography. This has become more of the norm rather than the exception. This is one of the main factors that lead us to the place where our careers start defining who we are. I purposely started this golf hole with this point, where I quoted above;

> *"Be careful not to build an unbreakable bond between what you do for a living and who you are as a person. All that matters is the latter. However, one who endeavors to build this bond in reverse order opens the door to limitless possibilities."*

This is a very tangled web that many of us get caught in. The reason we do is because the "spider" that spins this web is difficult to determine. Like I said above, it's a multitude of items that just find their way into our lives, and our affect our decisions. This is prevalent is all aspects of our lives, but especially in our careers. So, what do we do about it? How do we get to the point where we end up working in an environment that is a natural fit to the type of person we were always meant to be. Well, I would say that a great place to start would be to clearly identify with your strengths and weaknesses.

My guess is that it's best to start off with your weaknesses, as these are far easier to determine. For example, if you are "tone deaf" I would imagine that choosing a career in music wouldn't be a wise choice. So, what are your weaknesses? I would just focus on the glaring weaknesses (or fears), like the one I mention above. This should really be a short exercise, mainly because we never want to spend too much time on the "negativity" associated with weakness. Don't get me wrong, it's important to identify what they are, write them down, and keep them close at all times when making decisions. Not only career decisions, but all decisions. Again, do not beat yourself up over this…just clearly identify with what they are, and move on. For example, a weakness of mine is that I am not very technically sound. Therefore, I would not choose a career in computer science. Even if I was offered a great job, through a friend, as a computer technician, I would set myself up to fail due to my lack of interest, skill, or expertise. Another weakness of mine is that I have never been really good with numbers. Math was definitely my most difficult subject in both high school and college. So, again, I would not be successful as an accountant or in any other position that would require me to use numbers and be analytical.

I remember, early in my mortgage banking career, I considered joining the Six Sigma program at the bank I worked for. I was a very eager employee, had a very strong work ethic, and always have enjoyed learning and trying new and exciting things. However, once I realized all of the numbers and calculations that were necessary to become a Black-Belt (which sounded really cool) in Six Sigma, I knew it was not for me, and eventually choose not to take that path. In hindsight, I think that was a wise decision. The bottom line here, folks, is that we should really do the opposite of what we are usually taught on this topic. It's very typical for people to focus on their shortcomings. Not all of us are Rudy Ruettiger, the 23 year old groundskeeper at Notre Dame, who overcame his physical and athletic abilities...and made the football team as a walk on, and was the inspiration for the fantastic film, *Rudy*. It was a great story, but really plays into the old saying ... *"you can be anything you to be, if you just try hard enough."*

Be careful here, folks...because this statement is just not true. If it were, I would be playing in the NBA right now, playing for the Knicks...and they wouldn't be in last place.

Enough about the negatives...let's focus our efforts where they should be...on our strengths. You see, as Tom Rath states in his awesome book, *Strengths Finder 2.0*:

> *"You cannot be anything you want to be...but you can be a lot more of who you already are."*

I love this quote. It flows perfectly with our quest to "create" a more rewarding and fulfilling life. You see, we ARE in control; we just need to concentrate on the right things. The old saying "accentuate the positives" couldn't be truer when it comes to your career path. One interesting point here is that it's sometimes very difficult for us to actually determine our true strengths.

There are many assessments one can take to uncover this vital information, but the best I have seen lies in the aforementioned book, *Strengths Finder 2.0*. This book is excellent, and its sole purpose is to help you identify with your strengths.

You are provided a code in the book, which guides you to a website where you take an assessment. After you take the assessment and input your code, you get your results. The assessment focuses on your natural talents, and the results are derived by evaluating the answers to a series of detailed questions. It measures thirty four themes of talent determined by The Gallup Organization as those that most consistently predict outstanding performance. Themes that describe your personality (strength traits)....like: Achiever, Analytical, Communication, Maximizer, Consistency, Focus, Includer, Responsibility, Strategic, Discipline, and others. I really enjoyed this exercise and I was very pleased with my results.

To help you identify if this will be a good exercise for you, I will share the short version of the results of my assessment. Here are my *Top Five* strengths:

Connectedness

Shared Theme Description - People who are especially talented in the Connectedness theme have faith in the links between all things. They believe there are few coincidences and that almost every event has a reason.

Your Personalized Strengths Insights - By nature, you bring a much more optimistic perspective to life than many people do. Why? You feel closely linked to other members of the human family. Knowing you are not alone in your sufferings or joys fortifies you. Driven by your talents, you conclude that your life is more meaningful and you are happier when you can dedicate yourself to something of importance to humankind.

Positivity

Shared Theme Description - People who are especially talented in the Positivity theme have an enthusiasm that is contagious. They are upbeat and can get others excited about what they are going to do.

Your Personalized Strengths Insights - Because of your strengths, you enjoy discovering as much as you can about the people you meet. You are friendly and enjoy socializing. You quickly put at ease those you are meeting for the first time or the tenth time. By nature, you naturally gravitate to situations where you can be your true self. You feel life is wonderful when people listen as you share stories about your successes, failures, talents, limitations, hopes, or fears.

Maximizer

Shared Theme Description - People who are especially talented in the Maximizer theme focus on strengths as a way to stimulate personal and group excellence. They seek to transform something strong into something superb.

Your Personalized Strengths Insights - By nature, you exhibit a heightened awareness of your talents. One of your top priorities is building upon these natural abilities to create strengths. You undoubtedly find opportunities to practice using your talents in new and different ways. Driven by your talents, you can introduce a spirit of optimism, energy, and enthusiasm to individuals and groups.

Responsibility

Shared Theme Description - People who are especially talented in the Responsibility theme take psychological ownership of what they say they will do. They are committed to stable values such as honesty and loyalty.

Your Personalized Strengths Insights - It's very likely that you experience pangs of remorse when you realize you failed to do something you promised to do. You feel awful when you do not do something correctly. You probably regret having compromised your basic values about right and wrong. By nature, you prepare for assignments by reading extensively. Your capacity for pulling together information from books, publications, correspondence, notes, or Internet sites serves you well.

Arranger

Shared Theme Description - People who are especially talented in the Arranger theme can organize, but they also have a flexibility that complements this ability. They like to figure out how all of the pieces and resources can be arranged for maximum productivity.

Your Personalized Strengths Insights - Because of your strengths, you might excel on teams whose members appreciate your ability to simultaneously think about several ideas, problems, or tasks. The more you have to juggle, the happier you may be.

As you can see, the descriptions are very detailed regarding the theme. They provide a general description, as well as personal evaluations based on your answers to the questions on the assessment.

Your turn: what are your strengths? If you already know, that's great. Do you utilize them daily in your occupation? There's a good chance that you fall into one of two categories.

- People who really don't know there true strengths
- People who do not incorporate their strengths into their occupation.

That's OK...it's the back nine ...remember? Maybe, now is the time to change careers...and change course. For me, that is exactly what I am doing. I have actually used all of my top five strengths throughout my career, but some more than others. For me, Connectedness is my number one theme. A theme I will continue to focus on throughout my back nine journey. Just the fact that you are reading this book tells me that I am on my way.

Back on the course. I can see that hitting a shot from a "plugged lie" in a sand bunker is clearly a strength for you. Incredible shot, my friends. Your golf ball almost went in the hole, and lies only three feet from the cup. All you have left is a short uphill putt for a par. Take your stance, take a practice stroke, and knock it in. Please keep in mind that it is very important to go through the same pre-shot routine on these short putts as you do on the long putts. Staying with your routine, will help you avoid mistakes, which we now know is very important as we make our way through the back nine"

Stroke 4 – What is your end-game? What does "success" mean to you?

OK, we have spent a lot of time on this hole evaluating ourselves, again. I hope that feels as good to you as it does to me. Self-evaluation is so awesome, and something we should continue throughout or lives. We will discuss this in greater detail on #17, as we play the Personal Growth hole. Hopefully, our evaluation of our careers (past and present) has provided each reader some insight on what needs to be done to align our careers with our strengths and our passions. It's never too late for a change. I'm forty five years old as I write this book, and I am getting involved with things that I have never done before. For example, this is my first book! I probably shouldn't brag about that, but the point here is that I identified through the "strength-finder" piece and other mechanisms, that I had a strong passion for writing. It started out as a series of e-mails to the sales people that I have worked with over the years, graduated into a series of motivation e-mails and a blog, and has evolved into what you are reading today. When I talk about your "end-game," I am really referring to your ultimate "goals" for your career. If they are aligned with who you really are, than your career goals may have some consistency with your life goals.

For me, that is exactly where I want to be. I am not there yet, but I am getting closer everyday. Everybody defines "success" differently. Most people equate success with money, stature, and/or possessions. Here's how Webster's defines success:

"Achievement of intention: the achievement of something planned or attempted"

There are a few more descriptions below this, like fame, wealth and power...but I like the first description the best.

Achievement of intention truly gives an aggregate view of what success really means. It encompasses all aspects of our lives, not just our careers. Yes, we will spend many years in the workforce, but that doesn't mean our success will be derived solely from our occupation. On the contrary, success has everything to do with who you become as a person. Which brings us right back to the same place, my friends. Right here, right now, the beginning of our back nine. These are the barometers will we use to determine whether or not we are successful on this back nine journey.

Well, we have nine barometers (components) to start with. We have already covered four, and we have five golf holes left to play. Ultimately, our success will be measured when we are through. It will be measured by the people we leave behind and in the end, by God. For it does not matter what we acquire, all that matters in the "mark" we leave behind.

Back on the course. Great par on this most difficult golf hole. You overcame some serious adversity on this hole, and still ended up with a solid par. You hit an excellent drive that cleared the hazard, avoided the water down the left, and executed a superb bucker shot that almost went in for birdie. Your "muscle memory" on this hole was admirable, and that memory helped you keep your focus on each shot. You really seem to be enjoying yourself, which is one of the main reasons we play golf, right? Keep these positive thoughts in mind; you will need it for the next hole. You are doing great, and I am really enjoying being your playing partner!

#14 – "Your one true authentic swing" - Par 5

"From the beginning of time there has been a predestined purpose for every single human being who has entered this world. Our first challenge is to have faith and to believe that this is true. Our second challenge is to find the right path that connects us to that purpose, and to be steadfast and strong while we stay on that path. And our third and final challenge is to never forget the first two."

—Tony Caico

On the course *– OK, back niners, #14 is the number one handicap hole on the golf course. This basically means that it plays the most difficult. It is a very long par 5, 575 yards from tee to green. The first shot is a blind shot over a very large hill with trees lining both sides of a very narrow fairway. Your second shot will most likely have to be a layup shot, unless you can carry the ball over 260 yards (which most players can't). It is also downhill, so landing on and holding the green will be a challenge. Keep in mind that the 14th green is also an island green, so the risk versus reward factor is greatly skewed towards risk. However, if you hit a solid tee shot and a good second shot, you can position yourself about 120-130 yards away for your approach to the green. There is a sand bunker in the back of this green, and again, water all around.*

This will require tremendous accuracy and precision. This green is also very small and fast, and the pin placement today is on the left front. Anything short has a chance of filtering right back down to the water in front. That's the bad news. Here's the good news. If you play this hole well, your overall golf game will improve and the improvements will carry over each time you play. You see, playing this hole is like building a foundation for your house. Once you learn how to master the individual components of #14, you will equip yourself with the necessary tools that will assist you in building the rest of your house. Everything will make more sense, and you will immediately feel more empowered. Your golf swing will feel smoother, your accuracy will improve, your ball will land softer, and your confidence will soar to new heights. Don't get too nervous; you will be playing this hole quite often, and you will always get another chance. The key will be for you to remember the things you are learning while you are playing #14, and to incorporate them into your overall game plan in an attempt to create your ultimate back nine. OK...here we go!

Stroke 1 - Spirituality

I'm quite certain that every human being at some point in their life questions the reason for their existence. In my opinion, this alone is the main reason why spirituality will be the most important component of this book, and ultimately, your back nine. Why was I born? What am I doing here? What is my purpose? What is my true path? What am I supposed to believe? Who shall I listen to? Who am I? Who am I supposed to be? The questions are endless, but all valid and purposeful questions to ask. You see, many people either stop asking those questions, or never really search hard enough for the right answers. Even worse, many of us are taught certain things at an early age, and never take the necessary time to find out for ourselves whether or not they are true and authentic for our lives. Every person is unique, and there is a plan, already predetermined (I believe) for every single one of us. Our quest then is to find out what that plan is, and what we need to do to execute that plan. In order to do that, we must first identify with who we are. To take it one step further in order to find out who we really are we must try and define what we believe. Here's where it gets really tricky. It gets tricky because what we believe changes over time. I know that is certainly the case for me.

My beliefs have changed many times over the years, but it really wasn't until the last several years where it all started to make sense to me. Sort of like what I mentioned during the "Knowledge" chapter, I wasn't ready to even investigate these items until I was face down with nowhere else to turn. But now that I have refueled my search and my quest for these answers, I am certain my life will never be the same. For me, it's truly become about God's purpose for my life. This is what I believe.

Sure, I have always believed in God, but I never really gave much thought to how this correlates with my life's purpose. For a while, I thought my life's purpose was to be a very successful business man, get married, have children, make lots of money, and the rest would take care of itself. Obviously, that didn't work out too well for me.

Why? Well, I believe now it's because I wasn't ready to relinquish myself to a higher power, or to the power of God. As you know throughout this book my strategy is to use my past experiences as a frame of reference, and my ideas and goals for my back nine in an attempt to provide guidance for myself and my playing partners. I do realize that my views on some components may not necessarily correlate with yours, and that is perfectly fine. I hope you feel the same way, as it's through our diversity and our quest for knowledge that we quite often find the answers to these questions. In fact, it's been through my study of different belief systems and religions that I found my true path, my true purpose. I will dive deeper into that as well as the different religions and beliefs later on this hole. But now's the time to pay close attention and learn as much as you can so you'll find the keys to this elusive spiritual path.

I have been focused and purposeful trying to find my true path and my actual relinquishment to a "higher power" proved to be the key that unlocked the chains. I knew this was a power that was beyond my control, beyond my thoughts, and sometimes even beyond my comprehension. I can tell you that relinquishing control (in my case, to God) has been one of the most empowering decisions I have ever made. I realize now that my job is not to be in control of everything. My job is was to identify with who I really am, what I really believe in, and to have faith that identifying with these items will lead me to my path.

Of course, I didn't always think like this—I felt kind of the opposite, actually. Like many people, for some reason I always had to be in control. I wanted to make my own decisions, because I thought that I knew everything. What a mistake! I was well spoken, strong-willed, intelligent, and very confident… or so I thought. I didn't need "spirituality" in my life; I had everything under control. Well, again, you can see where that led me. It led me to a very cold, dark, and extremely lonely place. I would not wish that upon any of you, but my sense is that many of you have been there. Some of you might actually still be there.

What I can tell you is that finding this "stillness" or "oneness" like Eckhart Tolle describes in *The Power of Now* is a feeling of real power. I would imagine this is a different feeling for each person, but I equate the feeling of finding this "peace" to finding God. That has made all the difference for me, and my vision has become crystal clear as a result.

A few months back, I read an awesome book that Tracey Stewart wrote about her late husband, the great Payne Stewart. This book moved me in ways I can't really describe. The story of Payne Stewart's life told by his beloved wife was a captivating story of promise, fulfilling dreams, tragedy, and spirituality. I will talk more about Payne Stewart when we get to the 19th hole, but let's just say he was one of my all time favorite golfers. When I read about his life through the eyes of his wife, I was moved by the spiritual transformation that took place in the last few years of his life. I was able to see comparisons between his life and mine. Payne wasn't always the most well-liked individual that graced the fairways. He was bold, brash, opinionated, and like many of us, didn't really have a functional filter built between his brain and his mouth. The difference between his early quotes and how he spoke in the later years of his life, after re-connecting with his faith and "true-calling" are remarkable. Like I described earlier about myself, it seemed like

Payne Stewart became a changed man in his later years. He talked differently, he acted differently, and there was a peace about him that he never had. You could actually see it in his face and in his actions. He admitted to this on many occasions in the years before his death, and it was reiterated in this great book, entitled, *Payne Stewart*. It was also very prevalent in an interview he gave on the Golf Channel in response regarding one of his good friend's bout with cancer.

Another one of my favorite golfers, Paul Azinger, was diagnosed with cancer about the same time Payne was reconnecting with his faith. During that interview with Peter Kessler (from the Golf Channel) Payne talked about the value of life, he talked about the importance of his family, the importance of his faith, and about the fact that golf was just a game. He talked about how God has a purpose for everyone, and that Paul Azinger's purpose was not yet fulfilled, which is why he ended up beating the cancer and later returned to professional golf.

Ironically, it would be Payne's life that would be cut short a few years later. We talked earlier about a path and purpose for our lives. We have talked about what we will leave behind when we are gone. Well, in my opinion, Payne Stewart's legacy will live on forever, for a few reasons. One, because he was a fantastic talent and golfer, with the absolute "purest" golf swing I have ever seen. But more important, because in his later years, he finally identified with who he really was, re-connected with his faith, and it showed through in his demeanor, his dialog, and even his golf game. In the last year of life, only a few months before his tragic plane crash, he won the U.S. Open (at Pinehurst) and was a participant in the most memorable Ryder Cup victory in history. Although his life ended way too short, I believe his purpose in life was fulfilled and will live on through his friends and family. Just a few days ago I was reading about his son, Aaron, who is now playing golf at Southern Methodist University, the same college Payne attended. I will be following that story closely, thanks to the impact this man (and this book) had on my life.

Regardless of your own personal beliefs, is there really a doubt about the importance of spirituality in our lives? The "reason" for our existence, which kind of says it all. What an interesting and fantastic topic to talk about, to study, and to ponder as we begin to create own ultimate back nine. After all, our desire to learn more about this topic (and others) is woven into the fabric of our beings from birth. We are all born with that curiosity to want to explore and investigate, but somewhere along the way we start to ignore our inner self. We doubt our beliefs and we lose our grasp on our search for spirituality. Our focus shifts to: who we think we should be, who we are told to be, who others want us to be, and we start taking pieces from other people we know in an attempt to fill our gaps. However, what we end up with is *all tiles and no grout.* What is the grout? The thing that ties it all together for us, my friends, our spiritual being. Our one true and authentic self. Bagger Vance said it best:

> *"Inside each and every one of us is our one, true authentic swing. Something we were born with. Something that's ours and ours alone. Something that can't be learned... something that's got to be remembered"*

> ***Back on the course.*** *Fantastic tee shot! That was, by far, your longest drive of the back nine, about 270 yards. You are set up in a good position at the top of the hill with a perfect view of the rest of the whole. Be careful not to be fooled by the beauty of this next shot. The green will appear much closer than it is due to the downhill nature of your next shot. However, it's still about 290 yards away to a very small green. The smart play would be to play a shot about 180 yards right down to the bottom of the hill. From there, you will be left with a short wedge to this island green. Be still, quiet your mind, trust your instincts, and stay focused.*

Stroke 2 – Education - The importance of investigating other religions and belief systems.

In order to make sure we tackle this component with the depth it deserves, it's critical that we ingest as much as we can regarding other religions and beliefs. If you recall a few holes back, we made a commitment to make sure that we never lose sight of our thirst for knowledge. Remember, as we age, our brain functions will slow down if we don't continue to feed them. When it comes to spirituality,

I can't imagine any more important place to keep our educational juices alive. Now, some of you may be saying "I have my beliefs from when I was raised, and those beliefs are the foundation of my life." That is great for you, and I commend you for your loyalty and commitment to your faith. However, just because you have been taught something regarding how you should believe, wouldn't you honestly feel better about your own beliefs if you had more than one reference point? After a thorough investigation, many people end up right back with their original beliefs. However, they usually feel better (and wiser) for spending the time to learn about the other belief systems.

In contrast, many others find something else in other belief systems that resonate deeper with them. They realize that what they were taught to believe and what they actually believe are not necessarily the same. They find peace and tranquility in another form of spirituality, and those new beliefs have helped them find their way. To be perfectly honest I am still trying to figure it all out, but for me, the former is truer than the latter. I have pretty much ended up where I started, and that is with God.

As I have previously stated, although my intention for this book is to be a reference guide for back niners, that doesn't mean I am an expert on any subject. I am learning just like you. I have figured much of this out for myself, but we all have areas that we need to constantly improve upon, especially when it comes to spirituality.

If you grew up on Long Island, New York, in the sixties like I did you were either Catholic or Jewish. We were Catholic, and overall, my religious experiences (at least in my youth) were very comforting and positive. I always believed in God, and I can remember a few instances from my childhood when I actually felt very close to God. I usually enjoyed going to church when I was young, unlike most kids my age. My brothers and sisters used to tease me about singing in the choir, and I also told them I wanted to become a priest someday. Of course, my mother totally supported this notion, which turned out to be the cause for more teasing from the siblings. The bottom line is that God was with me from the beginning, and he has truly never left me. I certainly left him for a while, and spent many days and nights with the other guy that resides a little further south. I'm not sure exactly when it happened, but I assume my desire for spirituality left as soon as I hit my teenage years, which I suspect happens to many teens. I was basically done with spirituality, and really didn't pick it back up with the focus it deserves until a few years back.

That amounts to about thirty years of spiritual barrenness. I pretended to be Catholic, but really never led a true Christian life, not even close. No wonder why my life ended up where it did. Once you leave your path, you wander in the woods with no true sense of direction or purpose. Where do you think you will end up? This is not an attempt to defend myself, but the Catholic Church really didn't offer much spiritual guidance for teenagers. When you are younger, it's not too bad, and actually pretty cool to receive some of the sacraments like your First Holy Communion and Confirmation. You get gifts, have parties, and somehow feel that you are growing up. Although, as I look back, I am sure that I never really had a relationship with God. Something that has changed for me now. I'm not really sure what to call myself these days, but I guess a Spiritual Christian would be the best way to describe how I feel.

I also believe that Catholics are Christians, a subject matter that is debated often among Evangelical Christians and Catholics alike. For me it's all about one's choice to worship, and one's choice to have a relationship with God. For Catholics, it's through rituals, organized masses, Sacraments, and other forms of strict conformity. I imagine that these are the items that no longer resonate with me, which is why I do not go to Catholic Church anymore. The bottom line is that everyone needs to find the spiritual path that connects them to their purpose. It can be found through many different mechanisms, but investigating this is a very personal back nine journey. What I believe is that everyone has a choice and that there is not one right religion or faith. Just because I choose Christianity doesn't mean I can't respect another person's view. That is my stance and I'm sticking to it. What do you believe? What is your faith? Have you changed faiths? Have you investigated other faiths to make sure yours are right for you? Do you think this should be an instrumental part of your back nine journey? How much connectedness do you have between your faith and your overall life?

Let's spend some time talking about some of the other major world religions. There are a plethora of religions and many variations of each. However, for the purposes of our learning and discussion, let's keep our focus on the five major world religions and talk just a little bit about each one. They are Judaism, Christianity, Islam, Hinduism, and Buddhism. These five religions make up about 80% of the world's population.

As you read through these descriptions, try to gain some insight into your own beliefs and how you can actually enhance what you already believe by digesting some of this awesome information. This is what happened to me as I started learning more. I can truthfully say that there are pieces of every single one of these religions that I have incorporated into my thinking and into my life.

JUDAISM is the world's oldest and is a religion of just one people: the Jews. They were the first to teach belief in only one God. Two of the other important religions developed from Judaism: Christianity and Islam. Jews think that God will send a Messiah to unite them and lead them in his way. Christians believe that Jesus was the Messiah. The Jewish people do not agree; they anticipate his arrival in the future. Judaism teaches that death is not the end and that there is a world to come, and details of the afterlife are not part of Jewish faith. The "Torah," the first of five books of the Hebrew Bible, is the most important Jewish scripture. It contains the basic laws of Judaism. There are over 18 million followers of Judaism scattered throughout the world, with most of them living in Israel. However, there are also over six million Jews living in the United States.

CHRISTIANITY is a faith based on the life and teachings of Jesus Christ. Followers are called "Christians." They believe in one God who created the universe and continues to care for it. Their God sent his son Jesus into the world to save humanity from sin and to make eternal life possible for them. That son was crucified on the cross to accomplish this purpose. Christians believe they can be delivered from sin through their belief in Jesus. If they repent their sinful ways, and ask Jesus into their heart, they will be forgiven and given eternal life. The Bible is the sacred book of Christianity. Christianity is divided into a number of individual denominations.

The Roman Catholic Church is the largest Christian denomination with over a billion followers worldwide.

ISLAM is the name given to the religion preached by the prophet Muhammad in the 600s A. D. He was an Arab born in Mecca and people of this faith believe that he was sent by God (Allah) to guide his people and be their messenger. People who believe these ideas are called Muslims. There is only one religion which has more followers worldwide than Islam: Christianity. The holy book of Islam is the "Koran.", and Muslims believe its words to be those of Allah himself, spoken to Muhammad by an angel. All Muslims are required to make a pilgrimage (trip to a sacred place) to Mecca at least once in their lifetime.

HINDUISM is one of the world's oldest religions. It was named for the Indus River in India where it began over 4,000 years ago. Hindus believe in many gods, numbering into the thousands. They recognize one supreme spirit called Brahman ("the Absolute.") The goal of Hindus is to someday join with Brahman. Until that union takes place, believers are in a continuous process of rebirth called "reincarnation." At death, the Hindu's deeds (karma) determine what the next life will be. Over two thirds of the world's Hindus live in India and Africa.

BUDDHISM was founded in India about 2,500 years ago by a teacher whose name was Prince Siddhartha Gautama. To his followers he was the Buddha ("Enlightened One"). At various times in the past, it has been a dominant religious, cultural, and social force in most of Asia. Today there are about 300 million Buddhists in the world; most live in Sri Lanka, southern Asia, and Japan. Buddhism states that existence is a continuing cycle of death and rebirth. Each person's position in life is determined by his or her behavior in the previous life. This is known as their "karma" (also a Hindu belief). As long as a person remains in this cycle of birth and death, he or she cannot be completely free from pain and suffering. To break out of the cycle, it is necessary to lose all desire for worldly things.

These five religions have many obvious differences, of course, but they share certain elements. Those are: (1) belief in a power beyond the individual; (2) accepted teaching of salvation (goal of a life after death); (3) a code of conduct; (4) use of sacred stories; and (5) religious acts and ceremonies.

Before I continue, let me also talk a little about **New Age** spirituality. This is a bit of a controversial discussion for many Christians, but I have drawn a tremendous amount of inspiration from authors like Eckhart Tolle, Deepak Chopra, Wayne Dyer, Carolyn Myss, and others. I'm not sure that all of these folks would classify themselves as "New Age," but the concept behind these beliefs has synergy with each of their writings and teachings.

Here's a little information on New Age. New Age basically promotes the development of the person's own power or divinity. When referring to God, a follower of New Age is not really talking about a transcendent, personal God who created the universe, but is referring to a higher consciousness within themselves. Highly eclectic, New Age presents itself as a collection of ancient spiritual traditions. It acknowledges many gods and goddesses, as in Hinduism. The Earth is viewed as the source of all spirituality, and has its own intelligence, emotions and deity. But superseding all is self. Self is the originator, controller and God of all.

Clearly, there are many differences between all religions and belief systems. What is so interesting is that the histories of each of these religions run very deep and wide, and there is so much to learn. Unfortunately, many of these differences have led to bloodshed over the years. Like I mentioned before, I am a Christian, but I am also a firm believer that none of us has the right to judge other people based on their beliefs. Remember, we are creating our own new version of our back nine that will lead us to enlightenment, purpose, and true happiness. I am here to tell you that you can absolutely pick up a few "nuggets" from each one of these religions that will help you tap into your own spirituality on your second half journey.

Back on the course. Another fine shot on this hole, my friends. A wise club choice and a smooth swing has you in fine position for your approach shot. You are a fast learner, and I believe, destined for back nine greatness. Stay in tune with this next shot, as it is one of the more challenging on the back 9. You have about 115 yards to the green, but you should choose a club that will put you in the middle of the green. Going for the pin on this shot could be very dangerous, as your ball could end up in the water. Oh, I'm sorry; I didn't mean to put a negative swing thought in your head. Take it out, keep your mind still, and execute the shot you were meant to hit all along. Go ahead!

Stroke 3 – God

As I mentioned on a few occasions, I have five children. For those of you who have children, I want you to go back for a second to the actual day they were born. For me, there is no other single moment of my entire life to date that I realized the presence of God greater than those five days. Those are by far the five best days of my life thus far. Watching my children come into this world was just an awesome and incredible experience for me, and I'm sure I'm not alone. Bottom line, I really can't get through a golf hole on spirituality unless I spend considerable time talking about God.

Again, the term God may mean something else to you, but God to me is the presence of a greater power in my life that is beyond words, thoughts, dreams, and consciousness. He is my one true source of light, my one true source of being. My children and I have a special connection and we often talk one on one about what and who is in your heart. "You and Jesus" we say…while we touch each other's chest. In recent days, this act alone brings me to tears, mostly because I've lost the opportunity to be with them every day. You see, being away from God led me down a path that took me away from my children. Well, I'm back now, and like we said before, "It's never too late."

I would like to take you back again to the introduction of this book. Don't worry, you don't to flip pages; I will take you there myself. Do you remember when I talked about my vision to write this book? Do you remember when I said I woke up the next day, and suddenly I had a new focus, and a new direction? Do you remember when I said everything was different and I was ready to take charge of my life? Well, that was all true. However, the part that I left out of the introduction is that it didn't stick! That's right, it just didn't last that long.

About two months later I fell back into another deep depression. Yes, I had a new job, and yes I was starting to do some writing and feeling better about myself. However, there was still something missing. Throughout this entire process, one of my good friends made it clear to me that she thought "God was missing" from my life. Actually, she told me that on the day we first met several months earlier, while I was describing my situation. "Where are you with spirituality? Where are you with God?" I told her that I really wasn't ready to address that part yet, and that I had been studying some other religions and reading Deepak Chopra, Eckhart Tolle, and some others in preparation for my writing. You see, I knew that the "spirituality" chapter was going to be an important one, and I knew I wanted to gain more knowledge. But I thought that I could do it the "old Tony" way, by taking control of the situation. Well…again…this wasn't working for me. I was heading south again, and you know who was there to greet me with open arms.

The Devil is very strong character and can grab hold of you very quickly, especially if he knows you well. Well, he knows me very well for sure and he was ready and willing to do some partying with me. He won that round. I slipped again and started drinking, over eating, and behaving poorly for about two months. I couldn't write, I stopped reading, and I was really disgusted with myself. I was so depressed one Saturday, I called my friend (the same one), and she insisted that I go to church the next day. She found a local non-denominational Christian church and knew some great people who agreed to meet me and welcome me to their church. I was in such bad shape, I said, "OK…I give…I'll go." What happened next I will never forget. On this day, I would come back to God. When I arrived at the church I was welcomed by some very friendly people who basically gave me the quick tour and *Reader's Digest* version of the church. I walked into the auditorium to some awesome sounding rock music. I thought, "OK…this is pretty cool…I can do this."

I grabbed a seat right up front, which is something I learned from my days in business, and settled in. After the music ended, the pastor came on stage with an Affliction tee shirt, jeans, and a pair of Chuck Taylor's. Again, pretty cool, I thought. You see, I always knew that I needed something more, something deeper, but I was always too lazy and preoccupied to venture out in search of something more meaningful. I just kept going to Catholic Church right up until the point where I just didn't get anything out of it anymore, and then I stopped going completely. Anyway, the topic of his discussion that day was "When Life Hurts." I'm sure I couldn't have picked a better day to come back to God, and I soon realized that it was no accident that I arrived that day. He talked about the struggles and hardships of life, and that God never really leaves us, it's us who leave God. Of course, I already knew this; I just was never willing to admit it and change. All I needed to do was to accept him again, start talking to him again, follow him again, and he will lead me where I needed to be all along. I honestly felt that the preacher was talking directly to me. I started balling like a little girl, and barely stopped crying the entire time. I didn't know anyone there, but I imagined I would have cried even if I did. The real kicker was when he started talking about his daughter.

The overall message was about when life hurts, and what you do to get through those difficult moments. You see, the pastor lost his 11 year old daughter in a car accident several years before. He was telling the story, and he was crying on stage. Not like Jimmy Swaggart or Tammy Faye Baker…these were real and authentic tears from a man who lost his flesh and blood. I was so moved, I am sure I have never cried that much in my entire adult life. I had such a range of emotions. I felt guilt (I still have my kids), shame (how could I have strayed so far from God), sorrow (for his loss), and joy (I still have a chance!!).

So, God is back in my life, or should I say I found God again. By the way, the song by the fabulous band the Fray, "I found God" was one of the songs they played at church that day. WOW…pretty cool… right? The Bible is now part of my reading again, and I am glad that it is. It's really an awesome book that you can draw wisdom from in almost any situation. A few weeks later, a friend of mine sent me an e-mail with a website link called: "The Bible on One Page."

As part of my self guided tour for your back nine, I will share the website:

http://www.jrsbible.info/bible.htm

What's even cooler is that there is a listing of "emergency phone numbers" to link onto when you are looking for extra spiritual guidance in particular areas of your life. All you do is click on the link, and it takes you to the section of the Bible that will help you through this concern.

I know that I still have a long way to go, and there are still many things that I question about my faith. However, I have a genuine sense of security now that I have found God again. I am certain that I will never lose sight of him again. I know this will help me become the man I was always meant to be, and certainly assist me in creating the best back nine that I could have ever imagined. I hope this was helpful for you as well, as you make you way through your own spiritual journey.

> ***Back on the course.*** *Very nice approach shot, my friends. You played a very smart and safe shot to the back of the green, and you are left with a downhill putt of about thirty five feet. Well done. The green has a steep slope from back to front, so you will need to hit this putt softly. However, it also has a severe left to right break. Therefore, you will actually need to have both the distance and the accuracy correct in order to execute this putt. It's time to put all of your putting knowledge together, as this could be an awesome opportunity for a birdie. Just think if you can birdie the most difficult hole on the course, your confidence will shoot through the roof!!*

Stroke 4 – Path and Purpose - It all ties together!

We started this golf hole talking about making the connection between our purpose and our path. Early this fall, I was running on my usual course, when all of the sudden something happened. I call it my "Bagger Vance" moment. For those of you who have not seen this movie (*The Legend of Bagger Vance*), you must go out and buy it today. It's an incredible story with two incredible actors, Will Smith and Matt Damon. The movie has some variations from the book as is typical for Hollywood, but the message is crystal clear. It's more prevalent in the book, but the character, Bagger Vance, is really a metaphor for God, and his task is to help the other main character,

Rannulph Junah, find himself again, and to help him find his "lost swing" or his "way back to God." Please keep in mind that this is my interpretation of this story, and it could possibly have a different meaning for you. As I indicated in the introduction (or at the turn), the basic messages in this story and the basic messages of this book that you are reading are quite similar.

It's about finding ourselves, remembering ourselves, and ultimately clearing the path that will lead each of us to our purpose in life. A purpose that, again, has been predetermined by someone in a very high place. All we have to do find ourselves and the rest will take care of itself. There is a part in the movie, towards the end, where Junah is lining up his putt on the 18th and final hole of the match. His two competitors (Bobby Jones and Walter Hagen) have already pared the hole and Junah needs to make his putt to tie the match. It's a very long putt, about thirty five feet or so (sound familiar?). Right before he is ready to strike the ball, a light shines down from above. The light (from heaven in my view) shows him the exact path that the ball will need to travel down towards the hole. His vision all of the sudden becomes crystal clear as he strikes the ball on the perfect line and with the perfect speed. Well, you can imagine the result. He makes the putt and the crowd goes wild.

While I was running that day, something similar happened to me. Usually, when I run, my thoughts just go everywhere. I try and clear my head, but the quiet time also gives me time to reflect, ponder, and plan my next course of action. Well, this day was a little different. As usual, I was listening to my iPod, and the song, "Time of my Life" (by David Cook of American Idol fame) came on.

The song is about living every moment and letting go of the baggage of the past. It's about living every day like it's your last, and feeling that it is "your time." These are the feelings I felt while I was running and the words gave me a renewed sense of self that I hadn't felt in some time. Go ahead, Google the lyrics to this great song and soak it in. You'll be glad you did. As you can tell, I am a very sentimental and intense person, and I love music. I try and stay present and alert just in case there is an opportunity to grab something special. You see, you never really know when it's going to hit you or what will inspire you, so you must pay close attention at all times. As I started listening deeply and intently to the words of this song, all of the sudden, I saw the path in front of me getting clearer.

Yesterday it was a jogging path on the side of the road, but today it was "my path" and the light was shining right on it just for me.

What I realized at that moment in time was that *"This is exactly where I am supposed to be at this moment."* I started to have clarity about all of the trials and tribulations that I was going through. I now knew that I was supposed to go through all of that, in order to get me right back to place I was always meant to be. That place was here...now...searching my soul for a better life. That path entails writing a book, trying to heal, learning as much as I can about myself in an attempt to get to my purpose. What is my purpose? My purpose in life is to help people. My purpose in life is to add a significant contribution to as many people as I can. When I look back upon my career, I have actually done that on many occasions. But the difference is now I live with purpose, with focus, and most importantly, with authenticity. What is my vehicle that will help me fulfill this purpose? Well, I imagine it will be many things, but you are reading one, this book. This book which has become my own personal healing mechanism and I pray will be helpful to all those who hear my story and read my words. This is my true passion, my path, my reason for existence.

God is leading the way now, and he has helped me see this vision. Do I still have struggles? Absolutely! My life is still very hard, but I live much more peacefully now knowing that I have a purpose and knowing that I am putting the wheels in motion to fulfill this God-directed purpose. As Darren Gee so eloquently says in his book, *The Seven Principles of Golf:*

"Trust your instincts, find your way, and search your soul."

Deep down, we all know where we are supposed to be. Our innate wiring is to identify with ourselves and to follow our instinctive nature. The problem is we lose focus on how to do this because of all of the other "noise" in our lives. If we all just sat down and contemplated this for a second we will realize this and say to ourselves, "Yes, this is right, I do know where I am supposed to be and I do know who am

I suppose to be." Now, all we have to do is go out and do those things and be that person. Begin to trust yourself again, and your back nine will be everything it was meant to be.

You may be asking; "OK...I get it, but how do I actually get there...how do I actually put these items into play...and how do I ultimately tie all of these things together?" That's a great question, and I will conclude this chapter by offering some practical advice on the things that have helped me. A few months back, I ordered the movie, *The Secret*. It's an awesome piece that focuses on the positive flow of the universe and how we can each create our own success and happiness. There are two items in particular that I picked up from watching the short video presentation of *The Secret* that have helped me on my recent quest to improve. After all, that is what we are in search of, correct? The two items are: Vision Boards and Affirmations. A vision board is basically a self-made collage of all of the things you are searching for in your life. For example, on my vision board I have the following:

- A picture of each one of my children
- A picture of the type of home I will live in
- A picture of the type of car I will drive
- A picture of a clubhouse and a pool in the community I will live in
- A picture of a fantastic golf course...my home course!!
- A picture of me after I lost thirty pounds a few years ago
- A copy of the outline to this book; *My Back Nine*
- A picture of me and Jennifer Aniston (just kidding... that's not really there ☺)

I have strategically positioned my vision board right in front of me on the wall across from my desk. I look at it every day, and it helps keep me stay laser focused on my goals and dreams for me and my children. The other self-made document that I look at every day is a listing of my daily affirmations. The affirmations are more of a daily exercise, whereas the vision board is a peek into the future. My daily affirmations change from time to time, but here are the current affirmations that I read each day:

- Everyday...I am working on improving my life
- Everyday...I am working on improving my health
- Everyday...I am working on thinking positive thoughts
- Everyday...I am working on deepening my faith
- Everyday...I am working on improving my relationships
- Everyday...I am working on being a better father
- Everyday in every way...I am getting better

Bottom line, both of these exercises have helped me with my focus on staying on the right path. Although I continue to investigate this from all angles, I am very thankful to have found my purpose and I believe I am connecting closely with the path that will lead me there. Like I said, I certainly don't have it all figured out yet, but I am getting closer and getting better each day. What about you? Do you think these things will work for you? Go ahead...try them...what do you have to lose? Remember the old saying:

> *"If you keep on doing what you have always done.....you will keep on getting what you've always got."*

If what you are getting is not satisfying to you, my recommendation is to start with these simple tasks and see if they help lead you towards your path and purpose.

> ***Back on the course***. *Well, congratulations. It looks as though the light has shined down on your path to this hole, and you have made your birdie!!! I am so very proud of you. You are on your way to a fabulous back nine, and you have just mastered to most difficult hole on the course. You are two under par, with three pars and two birdies. Your golfing future looks very bright. All you have to do now is navigate four more holes on this back nine. Try not to get to overconfident, because you know where that leads. Keep steady and play one shot at a time. Stay in the present!*

#15 – "You're on the tee" - Par 3

"Most of us can learn to live in perfect comfort on higher levels of power. Everyone knows that on any given day there are energies slumbering in him which the incitements of that day do not call forth. Compared with what we ought to be, we are only half awake. It is evident that our organism has stored up reserves of energy that are ordinarily not called upon:-deeper and deeper strata of explosible material, ready for use by anyone who probes so deep. The human individual usually lives far within his limits."

—William James

On the course - *This hole is a short par three, about 165 yards in length. There is water in front and on the right side of the green, and there are two sand bunkers in front. #15 is ranked as the easiest hole on the course, but don't let that fool you. Your tee shot needs to stay left, as the slope of the green flows from left to right. Any shot that hits the right side of the green has the potential of going into the water. It may be surprising to you that this hole seems so much easier than the others, and it's almost like it doesn't "fit" on the back nine. However, you will soon see that playing this hole correctly will help you fill "the grout in the tiles" on other holes (not only today) but every time you tee it up. #15 may be short and a bit easier than some of the other holes...but* *the importance of this hole is a critical piece to your back nine. Be sure to choose the right club, and err on the side of "longer is better" because of the water hazard in front. This hole may seem a bit unusual to you, but the message will become crystal clear as soon as you stand on the tee. After all, you are first up, since you birdied the last hole.*

Stroke 1 - Leadership

When most people think of leadership, they usually don't think of themselves. They think of their boss, their coach, their teacher, or some other person who has been an influential person in their life. One of the items that we'll discuss in this chapter will center on the fact that "everybody" is a leader...and that leadership should be a major component of our lives. Isn't it true that we ALL take on a leadership role at some point in our lives? We become leaders of our families, leaders at work, leaders in our communities, and leaders in many other areas of our lives. But most importantly, we need to learn to lead ourselves. After all, we are talking about our back nine here. We are working on creating the lives we were always meant to live. Who is in charge of these decisions? Who is in charge of our lives? Yes, we are, and this is the type of leadership we want to dive into, right now. We need to understand this completely and act upon our findings if we are to reach our full potential. Many of us already know how to lead. Some of us are great at leading others, and some of us do a better job leading ourselves. For me, historically it has been the former.

It's funny, when I relate this to golf, the result is very similar. I have always been very good at teaching others to play, and giving them tips and strategies on how to improve their games. However, when it came to my own game, I never really focused on the mechanics of my own swing. Therefore my results were usually the same, mediocre. I could lead others on the golf course and on the job, but leading myself, now that was a different story.

I have been in a leadership position throughout my entire career. Even when I started at the bottom of an organization, I quickly rose to the top. I have studied leadership in detail for the last fifteen years of my life, and have a library filled with books on leadership and coaching, mostly in the sales arena. If someone were to ask me over the last ten years or so…"What is your greatest strength?" I would respond with "Leadership." I felt like I had that pegged, and that all of my study, reading, and practical use made me a very effective leader.

Was I right? Well, not really. Although others would describe me as an effective leader, I believe that I missed the boat on this one due to one critical factor. I will talk about that in a minute. A few holes ago, in the "Career" section, we talked about our strengths and weaknesses, and how we should really dial into to what they are as we try and ascertain what we should really be doing for a living. I gave you an example from the *Strength Finder* survey of my top five strengths. Interestingly enough, leadership was NOT one of them. This was a real shocker for me. There is no way that leadership should be missing. What went wrong?

Like I mentioned before, I was pleased with the overall results of the Strength Finder survey, but I was still confused why leadership wasn't there. After all, this is how I "defined" myself. I was so confused that I went and took the survey again. Guess what…the results were identical. The same five strengths came up, and leadership was not one of them. Needless to say, I was, again, shocked and confused. I really started thinking deeply about why I really wasn't the leader I thought I was. Then it hit me, all at once. The reason why leadership didn't show up as one of my strengths was that I wasn't the leader of Tony. I wasn't leading myself or my life. I started to tie all of the missing pieces of my life together, and realized that I was just posing as someone else. We will talk more about this in the Self Awareness section, but let's just say this was a huge wake up call for me. I immediately came to grips with the fact that you cannot honestly lead other people, unless you first lead yourself. Like the quote above states, I was only half awake. I wasn't leading myself, nor was I leading an authentic life. I was lying, cheating, posing, manipulating, showboating, abusing my body, disrespecting women, disrespecting my loved ones, gambling, etc.

How could I (or anyone for that matter) be a truly effective leader if I was doing all of these things behind the scenes? That's an easy question to answer, you can't and I wasn't. This is why leadership didn't show up under my top five, but my hope is that when I take this survey again in the future, it will. You see, I'm learning to lead myself. That is the point of this entire book; taking a long look inward in an attempt to rebuild and claim what is truly ours, which is a life of happiness, honesty, and abundance. However, it all starts with us leading ourselves, making good decisions, and paying attention to everything we do.

At the core of leadership lies two very critical elements which should be part of our back nine foundation, Truth and Character. If you are not being honest with yourself or others, than there is no way you can develop true leadership. Of course, not telling the truth and being honest lie at the core of one's character. We will talk more about character on the next shot, but honesty only comes in one form, consistency.

You can't be honest sometimes; you must be honest all of the time. Sure, not everyone is perfect, and we will sometimes falter. We all fall short, only God himself is perfect, we are not. But we can try to maintain a posture that includes honesty and integrity, with ourselves and others. This is certainly where I fell off course. I just wasn't honest with myself, and everything else fell apart around me. But I am learning, I am trying, and I am getting closer to being more authentic as each new day passes. I can tell you that just trying and making the commitment feels good, and I know I am on my way to being the leader I was meant to be. A leader for God, a leader for my children, a leader for my family and friends, and a leader for myself. When you develop into the leader you were always meant to be, everything else comes into focus and you start to realize your full potential.

As I mentioned earlier, I am a big fan of Vince Lombardi, and I will conclude this tee shot on #15 with the following quote on leadership. It's a perfect quote for the leadership story I just told you about myself, and I hope it will resonate with each of you:

"Leadership rests not only upon ability, not only on capacity; having the capacity to lead is not enough. The leader must be willing to use it. His leadership is then based on truth and

character. There must be truth in the purpose and will power in the character."

Back on the course. *Nice shot...you guys can really play. I thought you said you haven't played in a while. Well, I would say I don't believe you, but that would not be appropriate since we just spoke about truth and character. Your ball has landed on the back left portion of the green, exactly where you should be. You have a challenging downhill putt that will require a nice touch. There is not much break on this putt, but it is lightning fast...so be gentle. My suggestion would be to nestle down close to the cup, online, and hope it trickles into the hole. Don't go after this one aggressively. If you do, you could end up with a lengthy par putt.*

Stroke 2 – Let's break it down – Key components of Leadership

There are many different components that make up leadership, but let's stay focused on three relevant items that have the most synergy with creating our ultimate back nine outcome. These are: *character, responsibility, and significance.*

We will break down each of these in detail, and ultimately work together on mixing up a cocktail of leadership potion that will set us on the right path on this short par 3. As I mentioned, I have an unending list of resources right here on my bookshelf on leadership. I feel very targeted and focused on this topic, especially because I now know the true meaning of leadership. I have already read all of these books, but as I perused through them again in preparation for this chapter, I had a greater sense of awareness on the subject matter. I used to read these books to gain an edge on my competition and to get tips on sharpening my skill set to help me lead my teams better. I have to say, that this really did work for me, and I did enjoy a great deal of success in leading teams.

However, I didn't have the insight that I do now, and my motives, although authentic at the time, we are not based on a firm foundation of trust and character. As you look back on your front nine, what was it about your leadership abilities that you would like to change? That's what this is all about, folks. OK, let's jump it together:

Character – Where do we start with character? Deep inside is the best place. What do we value? What occupies our thoughts? The old saying by Ralph Waldo Emerson, *"A man is what he thinks about all day"* is really what this is all about.

For me, the thoughts that occupied my mind throughout much of my day were not healthy. They got me excited, they got me charged up, but they were superficial in nature, and eventually landed me in a scalding hot caldron. You see, character begins on the inside, at your very core. The things we think about and the things we value really determine the type of person that we are. Is that true for you? Is there something about your thought patterns that you wish you could change? That's OK, this is very common. Training our minds to think differently is sometimes very hard to do. But just because it's hard, that doesn't mean that you can't do it. This has been, and continues to be a very difficult thing for me to do. I have contemplated on many of the aspects of the book, *The Secret*, by Rhonda Bird, and the concepts have really helped me. The basic premise here is that if you focus your mind on positive thoughts and positive things, this is actually what your life will become. On the contrary, if you focus on the negative, you will have more negative things enter your life. It takes time to build that "strength of mind," but this one fundamental premise is critical to capturing your true path and ultimate back nine potential. Positive thoughts will help build your character, but they must be followed up with positive actions. The following American Indian quote, that I just heard again the other day, has really helped me over the last year or so:

"Inside of me there are two dogs. One of the dogs is unhappy, insecure and full of doubt. The other dog is joyful and confident. The unhappy dog fights the joyful dog all the time. When asked which dog wins, he said, "The One I Feed the Most."

We all have the choice of which dog we want to feed. If we focus on feeding the joyful dog we set ourselves up for more opportunities to build our character.

Two of my favorite books I have read (one older and one just recently) both start off with the topic "character" in their first chapter. I believe they did this because character is the foundation for the house, and I have followed suit by making it my first key discussion item on our second stroke. In Tony Dungy's book, *Uncommon*, he talks about character while discussing the larger topic of "building your core," or your foundation. He starts off the chapter on character by using an example of the 1998 football draft. Of course, as you must have figured out by now, I am a huge sports fan, so whenever I can get a point drilled into me by using an analogy from sports, my ears seems to open up a bit wider. This case was no different.

The Indianapolis Colts were faced with a decision of who to choose as their top draft pick in the 1998 NFL draft. They boiled it down to two choices, Ryan Leaf and Peyton Manning. In hindsight, Manning seems like the obvious choice, but at the time there was a great debate over who was better. They were equally talented on paper, but the ultimate decision came down to a question of character. No disrespect to Ryan Leaf, but Peyton's quiet private life, work ethic, and love for the game tipped the scales in his favor. The rest, as they say, is history. Bottom line is "what you do is not as important as how you do it." The next two chapters in Dungy's book are on honesty and integrity, both by products of a strong character. The other book I was referring to is John Maxwell's, *The 21 Indispensable Qualities of a Leader.* I love this book, and have read it several times. Mr. Maxwell's writing is very straight forward and to the point, and he does a great job using analogies as well as relating topics to everyday life. The first Quality of a Leader, according to Maxwell is Character. To elaborate more on my point above regarding the fact your character determines who you are, this chapter dials in deeper. He goes on the say:

"Your character determines who you are. Who you are determines what you see. What you see determines what you do. That is why you can never separate a leader's character

from his actions. If a leader's actions and intentions are continually working against each other, than look to his character to find out why."

WOW...I just had another incredible "ah-ha" moment about myself. This describes my old life to a tee (no golf pun intended). This is why I have lived so many years with a sense of insecurity that surrounded my life. Inside, I felt like I never fit in anywhere, even though I displayed a strong exterior. Bottom line, my character was weak, and the weaknesses of my character infiltrated every aspect of my life. What about you? Is it time to "cleanse your character?" Well, there is no time like the present to start leading a better life. Certainly, we all have character flaws, but at your very core, are you comfortable with your overall character? Interesting item to contemplate, right? Well, the good news is that this is your own version of your back nine, and you can change anything about yourself that you want to. All you need to do is focus on feeding the right dog. Remember, talent is a gift, but character is a choice!!!

Responsibility – This seems like an obvious component to evaluate when we talk about leadership, but there are many different variations of responsibility. Another word we could use here could be accountability. Clearly, the two go hand in hand, but both are critical to developing the leadership potential for your life. Here's how *Webster*'s defines responsibility:

"The quality or state of being responsible: moral, legal, or mental accountability"

Being a responsible person requires character, discipline, honesty, integrity, and morality. This is an interesting concept for me, and I believe that this "responsibility" has been acting like a moral compass for me throughout my entire journey. Certainly, the act of being responsible will be a key element as we improve our respective back nine's. But if I really think long and hard on this topic, responsibility was instilled in me many years ago. You see even though I acted irresponsibly in so many aspects of my life, I still held on to my view of responsibility regardless of what I was going through at the time. I can honestly say that even though I now believe that I was not acting like a good person, I always thought (deep inside) that I was a good person. I was still responsible in many areas of my life. I always tried to be a good son to my parents, a good father to my children, and a good friend to all of the people in my life…both personally and professionally.

A testament to this is that I have built an extensive network of individuals that I have kept in touch with for many years, and I have built a tremendous amount of incredible relationships. It seems to me, that I kept most of my bad habits to myself, and I think this is because I always had a sense of responsibility in the back of my mind. I was also very responsible in my career, and I was a recipient of many awards, promotions, and large commission checks as a result. My ego was very large, but I also had a strong sense of pride for my name, and I worked hard (on the surface) to keep that intact. Even now, after all of my problems, I am confident that my name is still good, and I have kept my head held high even throughout these very difficult years. In contrast to the missing strength of leadership on my Top five strengths, interestingly enough, responsibility made it on the list. I was pleased to see that, and I now realize this is all unfolding just the way it was supposed to unfold. That is a very gratifying feeling, my friends.

Let's switch gears for a minute, and talk about the unpopularity of leadership. Sometimes being a responsible leader means making tough and unpopular decisions, both in your personal and professional life. Whether it's disciplining your children, or making tough decisions at work, a true leader take on this responsibility with determination and focus. In Colin Powell's, *Leadership Primer* presentation, he describes what this means:

> *"Good leadership involves responsibility to the welfare of the group, which means that some people will get angry at your actions and decisions. It's inevitable, if you're honorable. Trying to get everyone to like you is a sign of mediocrity: you'll avoid the tough decisions, you'll avoid confronting the people who need to be confronted, and you'll avoid offering differential rewards based on differential*

*performance because some people might get upset. Ironically,
by procrastinating on the difficult choices, by trying not to
get anyone mad, and by treating everyone equally "nicely"
regardless of their contributions, you'll simply ensure that
the only people you'll wind up angering are the most creative
and productive people in the organization."*

This has always been a tough one for me. I was pretty good at making tough decisions, but I also wanted everyone to like me. Bottom line is that you need to have balance and consistency here. Nobody likes a leader that takes them on the roller coaster. So, whether you're at home or on the job, try and keep your responsibility radar focused on the result, and that should help you stay consistent. Where do you stand on responsibility? Do you consider yourself a responsible person? Are there areas of your life that you have left behind due to lack of responsibility? Maybe, it's your health, your relationships, your family, your education, your career, your faith, which basically covers all of the key life components we have discussed thus far. We each have the responsibility to improve upon all of these items if we plan on being the best we can on the back nine. Isn't it fantastic that we can tie all of these things together? It makes the process that much more enjoyable and obtainable once we realize that we are fully capable of doing all of these things…and that the result will be that we will be living more rewarding and fulfilling lives.

Significance – I have to be honest, I was waiting for this one. This one single word resonates with me more than any other word these days. As a matter of fact, if you were to ask me to serve up one word that describes who I am and what I want my life to be about, it would be *Significance*. Again, I believe that my purpose in life is the following:

*"To make a significant contribution to as many people as I
can, through my writing, coaching, relationships, and faith.
The centerpiece of my purpose is being a father to my five
children, and to make sure they have the best chance to live
a life of significance."*

John Maxwell has many excellent books on Leadership, but the *21 Irrefutable Laws of Leadership* is probably his best seller. His first quote underneath the book title says:

"Follow them and they will follow you." Now, that is as powerful as it is simple. This is something that I truly believe, and it has been this basic premise that has served as my leadership barometer for the last twenty years. Like I said, even though I made a plethora of mistakes, I always stayed focused on helping others, and I have used this philosophy as my primary source of influence over the years. The difference now is that I have a deeper understanding of the word *influence*. If you would have asked me the question above about the one word that would describe me, up until a few years ago, that one word would have been "influence." However, my overall character was weak, and deep inside I lacked the confidence that I needed to be authentically influential. I now plan to develop synergy between my old word (influence) and my new word (significance) just by keeping my focus on the latter. I truly believe that my influential powers will rise to new heights because of the new authenticity that is attached. In similar fashion to the first quote in Maxwell's book, Tony Dungy's book that I mention before (*Uncommon*) has a similar "first message."

As soon as you open his book, on the first page there is ONE sentence that describes the entire premise of his book:

"What does it take to live a life of significance?"

Not only does he begin the book with this statement, he concludes the book with the last chapter entitled Significance. He goes on to ask:

"Have you figured out what God has placed you here to do, and are you doing it to the best of your abilities? Therein lies the answer to significance."

I don't know about you, but this statement gives me chills. It gives me chills because, right now, while I am writing this sentence in the pages of *My Back Nine* I feel that I am fulfilling this purpose.

I am following my pre-destined path and working on leading a life of significance. Everyone needs validation and I am no different from you. Another form of validation comes to me from the following quote from Booker T. Washington:

"Success is to be measured not so much by the position that one has reached in life as by the obstacles which he has overcome."

I am living this quote right now, making a comeback, writing a book, and doing everything I can to make my life better.

What about you? What is your significant purpose? What is your ultimate scorecard that you will use to measure your life? If you don't have one, feel free to borrow this one from Mr. Dungy's book. I'm sure he won't mind, and it will serve you well.

I would be remiss if I didn't mention Lou Holtz in my discussion about Significance. After all, it was during a speech he gave at a business conference a few years ago when I really "latched on" to the concept of significance. I will conclude this stroke with the quote that makes up the last paragraph of his awesome book, *Wins, Losses, and Lessons*. Here it is:

"I don't think about the wins and losses these days, so I hope no one remembers them when they think of me after I'm gone. I want the great games to be remembered for the players who played in them, not the short, skinny man who paced the sidelines. I don't want to be known for the successes I had as a coach, or as a public speaker, because success dies. Significance – helping others to better their lives through word and deed – lasts forever. The only thing I hope is that when I die, someone says, that Lou Holtz was significant to a lot of people. It is the best thing that can be said of a person. I hope it will be said of me."

Back on the course. *Oh, man...that was close. Your putt just lipped out on the right edge. You struck the ball with perfect speed, and almost made another great birdie. You are now* *left with a very manageable uphill par putt from about three feet. This should be an east putt, but be sure to keep your head still and stroke the putt with authority.*

Stroke 3 – What type of Leader will you be?

Now that we have established the importance of leadership in our lives, how do we improve our leadership qualities and put this into back nine practice? Well, the first thing we need to do is evaluate our leadership positions. Father, spouse, boss, community leader, spiritual leader, and of course…leader of YOU. Then we need to determine the type of leader we will be, and it may very well be that our leadership roles will be different in each situation. For example, your leadership role as a parent will be different from your leadership role at work. You will certainly use the same qualities we have discussed (character, responsibility, significance), but you will use them differently depending upon the situation. As you could probably tell by now, I am a huge fan of John Maxwell. In my view, his views on leadership are expansive, and he has written many books on the subject. As a matter of fact I am reading his new book, *Put Your Dreams to the Test* right now. In this book, he mentions that his ultimate purpose and path in life is to coach and train leaders on becoming better leaders.

He has another great book, *The 360 Leader*, where he points out the fact that everyone is truly a leader, regardless of where they lie in the family or in the corporate structure. Each of us has a responsibility to lead, and it all starts with the basic understanding of leadership. My point here is that in order to identify with the type of leader you wish to become, you should investigate the different qualities of leadership itself. Let's go through these together, taken from Maxwell's book, *The 21 Irrefutable Qualities of a Leader*. As we go through each of these, take some personal accountability as to where you stack up on each one of these qualities. Go ahead and rate yourself on a scale of one to five, with one being the worst and five the best. This is something you can do on a recurring basis, as you improve in each of these areas. By reviewing each of these and seeing where we could use improvements, we will set ourselves up to be more effective leaders of our lives:

- Character – The most important quality of all
- Charisma – First impressions are lasting
- Commitment – Separates the doers from the dreamers
- Communication – Without it you travel alone
- Competence – If you built it, they will come
- Courage – One person with courage is a majority
- Discernment – Put an end to unsolved mysteries
- Focus – The sharper it is, the sharper you are
- Generosity – Your candle loses nothing when you light another's
- Initiative – You won't leave home without it
- Listening – To connect with their hearts, use your ears
- Passion – Take this life and love it
- Positive Attitude – If you believe you can, you can
- Problem Solving – You can't let your problems be a problem
- Relationships – If you get along, they'll go along
- Responsibility – If you won't carry the ball, you can't lead them
- Security – Competence never compensates for insecurity
- Self-Discipline – The first person to lead is YOU
- Servanthood – To get ahead, put others first
- Teachability – To keep leading…..keep learning
- Vision – You can seize only what you can see

I absolutely love this list, folks. It ties almost all of the components of our entire back nine right here in this compact space. If you refer back to the quote that started off this hole, you will note that if we dig deeper to find our true calling of leadership in our lives, we begin to awaken and start to utilize all of our God-given abilities and talents. It's through this awakening that we develop a hunger for more, a hunger for learning and growing. This is when our true path starts to reveal itself, through the leadership of ourselves and our ability to dial into all of the leadership qualities stated above. This will help us find our purpose, develop our priorities, uncover our passions, and ultimately help us build a bridge that will connect all three.

"In order to lead effectively, a person must first know how to live to make a difference in their own life, learn how to make a difference in other people's lives, and, most importantly, learn to make a difference through ethics and integrity."

—Don Soderquist

Back on the course. *OK…Sweet…another par. This may just be the round you have been waiting for your whole life. A round filled with positive energy, focus, determination, and phenomenal results. This was a solid par, with a great tee shot, a superb first putt and a solid and authoritative par putt. A job well done. Now, let's move on to #16.*

#16 – "Who are your golfing partners" - Par 4

"As the years go by it's the relationships in my life that I cherish the most. Daily interaction with family and friends, both old and new, provides the fuel that keeps our human engines idling at the precise level necessary for sustainability and growth. In the end, it's the imprint that we leave on others through our actions and our deeds that will determine both our legacy and our eternity."

— Tony Caico

On the course - *Compared to other holes on the back nine, #16 is fairly easy. Well, maybe "easy" isn't the most appropriate word, since those of us who play golf realize that those two words (easy and golf) rarely go together. Let's just say that if we continue the consistent play that we have displayed on holes ten through fifteen, we have a great chance of success on this hole. It's a fairly short par 4, measuring 385 yards in length. The fairway is very wide, so go ahead and take out your driver and give it all you have! There is water on the left, but it ends after about 150 yards. Therefore, a solid strike has no chance of hitting the hazard. Like all of the other holes on your back nine, you have many choices on #16. Remember, the choices you make on each stroke will determine your ultimate result. A solid drive will put you* *in excellent position for a short iron into an equally large green. The pin placement today is left middle, so you have an excellent opportunity for birdie. Let's play!*

Stroke 1 - Relationships

As a point of clarification, the first stroke on each of these important golf holes represents my "opinion" on why I view each topic as a key component of life. If you recall, the entire vision for this endeavor came to me when I awoke from a deep sleep, and the clarity of purpose I had about my thoughts that evening continue to this day. I actually came up with these nine components of life that evening and after much thought and deliberation, I have stayed consistent with these nine. It is my belief that if we carefully analyze, dissect, and improve on these nine life components, the second half of our lives will be joyous and wonderful. We will pull all nine of these components together when we discuss "happiness" on the 18th hole. After all, isn't that the point? For now, however, let's stay dialed into relationships, and how we can improve right here…right now.

Some may consider other topics as their top choices for the most important parts of their lives. Choices like: Love, Money (finances), or Faith (as opposed to Spirituality). I also consider these to be very important, and I try to incorporate all of these into one (or more) of the nine components. Let me provide an example of what I am referring to as it relates to this current chapter on relationships. When we draw comparisons to money and relationships, one could assume that in order to achieve financial success one must possess the ability to obtain, cultivate, and retain solid relationships. As Jeffery Gitomer says in *The Little Black Book of Connections*:

"Everyone wants to be rich. Although most people think being rich is about having money, rich is a description for everything but money. Rich relationships lead to much more than money. They lead to success, fulfillment, and wealth."

The point here is that regardless of what your own personal life component choices might be, my intention is that you can draw upon my evaluation of these nine and incorporate them into your individual lives as well as your detailed plans for your back nine.

I have been really looking forward to writing this chapter. As I mentioned in the quote above, relationships are among the most important things in my life. I'm sure many of you feel the same. However, have you ever thought about why?

The answer seems obvious, until we start peeling back the layers of the onion and dissecting our own relationships. We talked about family relationships on our first hole. We talked about all of the things we want to do to improve those cherished family relationships that we have lost focus of over the years. Well, the other relationships in our lives require similar focus and attention. How we handle our past, current, and future relationships has a direct impact on our level of achievement, fulfillment, and happiness. After all, isn't that what our entire day consists of? Dealing with people. Sure, we all deal with strangers each day, but most of our days are spent with the people we know and have relationships with. Isn't that what makes up most of our day? Do you ever have days where you are alone the entire day? Yes, we all need a break sometimes, but honestly, how do you feel when you spend the whole day alone? This really hits home for me. Over the last two years, I have spent more time alone than I have in my entire life. Due to the mistakes I have made, I do not get to see my kids everyday, and I live alone in a large house in the woods of North Carolina.

Sometimes I feel like Jack Torrence (played by Jack Nicholson), the caretaker in the great movie, *The Shining*. I'm just kidding of course, don't be frightened. Although this alone time has given me the chance to evaluate my life, my decisions, and many other things, the bottom line is that I have also felt a sense of utter loneliness for the first time. As many of you know, this is not such a great feeling. I do see my kids quite often, but as soon as I drop them off I usually get some uncomfortable separation anxiety, and I start to feel lonely again. Of all of the important relationships in my life, the relationships with my five children are the ones I cherish the most. I spoke of the importance of these relationships in the first chapter, but let's just say that a major part of my personal back nine preparation will be spent focused on my children. Yes, I have lost time with them over the last few years, but I am doing my best to make up for it. I'm doing my best to become a better father, a better person, and my children will be direct beneficiaries of those improvements. The impact I have on them and their lives is the absolute most important thing in the world to me, and I thank God everyday for these five blessings.

In addition, I have spent the last twelve years of my career away from home, traveling the country on business. I have met many people and developed friendships in almost every major city in the U.S. But now that I don't have that job anymore, and I don't have as many of those opportunities. More on those items later on this hole, but my point here is realizing the importance of each individual relationship. Now that I don't have the opportunity to actually see all of these people in person, I feel that there is a gaping hole in my life.

I am determined to fill that hole as part of my back nine preparation, even though I do not have the "vehicle" in place anymore due to my employment situation. My plan will include travel to spend time with these people again, and to continue to cultivate these very important relationships. Perhaps it will be to promote this book, in my quest to help others who have gone through similar trials. Either way, connecting with past friends and making new friends will be a large part of my back nine. How about you? How important are your relationships? How much time will you devote to work on improving yourself? How cognizant are you about meeting new people and developing new relationships? Should this be a more "present" part of your life?

Remember, we are charting our course for the second half of our lives. Do you think it's important to evaluate our relationships? Who do we spend our time with? How do we interact with our family members, our friends, our business colleagues? Shouldn't this be a major component of our lives? You know the answer…yes!

Back on the course. What a rocket!! Right down the middle. It seems like you have been waiting to let loose on a drive and you sure did on that one. This game isn't so hard…right? There is nothing like the sound you hear when you hit the "sweet spot". You can tell as soon as you hit it, just by the sound that it's going to be a beauty. You can hit the golf ball poorly all day (which is not the case today), and that ONE fantastic shot will keep you coming back for more. Well, you have hit many quality shots today, but that one may be your best drive. Well done. Your approach shot is only about 85 yards. Remember, there is a bunker in the back, so be sure to make the right club selection. Let's do it...together!

Stroke 2 – Relationship Status

Do you continue to renew and cultivate old relationships? Do you seek out new relationships?

As I began preparation for this chapter, it dawned on me that due to my constant focus on my relationships, my contact list continues to grow. The addition of Facebook, LinkedIn, and other social networking sites has helped me in that regard and I have now reconnected with many childhood friends though these new connection mechanisms. I really enjoy looking at pictures of their families, reading updates, and conversing with people that I may have never been in touch with if it were not for these new Internet sources. As I indicated earlier, I feel that my own personal back nine path involves making a contribution to as many people as I can. I hope to continue to touch new people through my communication and writing, but my plan is to start with the people I already know through school, work, and other places. This is why I just created a new distribution list through iContact, another networking medium. I have over seven hundred people on my distribution so far, and plan on adding many more through my work on this project, *My Back Nine*. You see, in similar fashion to all of the other nine key components, I will continue to make relationship building a part of my daily life on my back nine. I have also started a blog, where I post inspirational messages on a variety of topics. Feel free to check it out: www.myback9.com

Creating this blog has helped me grow as a writer, and has provided the fuel I need to keep my creative juices flowing. My blog has also helped keep my radar screen on in search of new sources of inspiration. What I find is that when I complete a new piece I feel very satisfied and energized, and this helps me stay focused on the truly important things in my life. In addition, due to the relationships

I have built with so many incredible people, I get constant feedback through comments on my blogs, e-mail, and phone calls regarding my blog posts. I must say that this feels good, even if the feedback isn't always exactly what I wanted to hear. Although I have worked very hard on my ego, a pat on the back and a sense of reassurance that my writing has an impact on others is a feeling that warms my heart.

In the Career section a few holes back, we discussed strengths and weaknesses and how we should incorporate them into our careers. Well, if you recall, one of my personal strengths was "connectedness." I love this word, as it sums up many of my feelings regarding relationships and life in general. It's also a word that will stay close to me as I work on my back nine improvements. After all, staying connected to all of these nine components will certainly help us achieve our goals with greater efficiency. As I ponder what it means to renew old relationships, I am reminded of a personal story of something that happened to me several years ago.

The lock feature on my cell phone broke, and the technician at the retail store could not fix it. After numerous tries and many calls to tech support, the phone could not be repaired. In addition, they could not retrieve any of my contacts. I had this phone for over ten years and almost everyone I know was in that contact list. What I thought was a dire situation, however, turned out to be a very rewarding experience. Although I did not have the contact list backed up (ouch), I did have e-mail addresses for most of the contacts. As I started e-mailing them to refresh my contact list, an interesting thing happened to me. I realized that over the years I have made many contacts with business associates that have actually become friends. My business contact list and my personal contact list had merged into one list. I was successful contacting and catching up with most of these people, and exchanged e-mails with the rest. I realized how important these people were (are) to me, and how important I was (am) to them. Through my re-connection with these folks, I started to get really pumped up about the past, present, and the future. You see, all of us have the power to "connect" with people. We control this. How cool is that?

The question is how many people do we really connect with? How many friends do we really have? In another great book by Jeffery Gitomer, *The Sales Bible*, he says:

"All things being equal, people want to do business with their friends. All things being not quite so equal, people still want to do business with friends."

To climb the ladder of success in business and in life, you don't need more techniques and strategies, you need more friends. Strong relationships lead to friendships. Think about that for a minute. How many friends do you have? Here's a great exercise for you to find out the answer right now. Get out a piece of paper, and list all of the people (other than family) that are in your life right now. Go to your e-mail list, your cell phone, and your Facebook account. Now, get another piece of paper and place the labels A, B, and C. You see where I am going with this, right? It's an old tried and true sales technique that really works. Let's say the following:

A – Very close friends. Friends that would bail you out of jail, lend you money in a dire situation, are there to support you if you have done something wrong, and offer you unconditional love regardless of the circumstances.

B – Good friends – Friends that you talk to quite often. Maybe business acquaintances that you have met over the years and you have become personal friends. People that you look forward to talking to and seeing and the feeling is reciprocated. People that make you feel good when you see them and talk with them, even if it's only once in a while.

C – Friends that you don't talk to or see that much. Friends that you were once acquainted with, but have lost touch with over the years. They are still in your contact list, but you do not really have the desire to talk with them, and again, the feelings are reciprocated. Maybe, these include some new

Facebook friends from high school or college that you have just re-connected with.

OK, here's the exercise. Your goal is to basically move the C's to B's, the B's to A's, and to maintain the A's. In this process, what you will find is that you will articulate who your friends are; this exercise also works in reverse order. In other words, some of your A's will become B's, your B's will become C's, and some of your C's will go off your list. That's OK; this is why the exercise is so powerful. In a sales environment, this works magically, and I believe it will work in the relationship environment as well. You may say, "I don't have time for this" or "a sales game is way different from real life." Maybe so, but just give it a try, and you will see the impact. We are talking about relationships here, how they affect our lives and how they will fit into our back nine. Anything we can add to our tool belt to help us in this cause will improve our outcome and lead us towards our desired results. You will be amazed, surprised, confused, and very curious after you complete this exercise. Trust me, in true back nine fashion, this exercise just took me forty five minutes. I basically took my personal e-mail list (about three hundred fifty or so) and printed it out. Here are my results:

A - Sixteen
B – One hundred and two
C – Two hundred and thirty five

I guess one could assume that there is only so much room in your life for a large number of really close friends, but I would challenge you to ponder that thought. For me, the glaring number on this list was my A's. I consider myself an excellent connector, yet I only have sixteen A's out of a possible three hundred and fifty three (or more if I include business, Facebook, and others). So, part of my back nine journey will include the process of moving C's to B's, and B's to A's. Sure, I will consider the A's very carefully, but wouldn't you agree that having more people close to you is a GOOD thing.

Back on the course. Another fine golf shot. Your approach shot has landed on the green, only about fourteen feet from the hole. You are left with an uphill putt with a slight break from left to right. Your putting has improved throughout this back nine, so you are totally prepared for this birdie putt. Keep your head down, pull the putter back low and slow, and accelerate through the shot. Good luck!

Stroke 3 – Relationship Building

If you are like me, you are carefully analyzing the results of the prior "relationship" experiment. You're probably thinking to yourself, "Where have I gone wrong?" or "What can I do to improve my relationship building skills?" That's a perfectly normal reaction, and we will dissect this together on this third stroke on relationship building. In order to build successful relationships we need to start with ourselves. As we pave our way through our back nine journey and improve on all of the components we are discussing, what we will find is that these improvements will become building blocks for our ability to improve, renew, and cultivate new relationships in our lives. As previously discussed, all nine of our life components fit together like a jigsaw puzzle. Let's review each of the components on holes ten through fifteen to uncover some key aspects of relationship building:

Family (#10) – If you recall part of our family discussion centered on our ability to dive back into our past and uncover some of the "reasons" why we have turned out the way we have.

If you're like me that proved to be quite a valuable lesson and awoke some sleeping giants inside that have been hiding for many years. As you uncovered those items in your own lives, you became more aware of how they have impacted you. That is a great first step, and if you accomplished that, you are already making progress. This progress will not only help you with your family relationships, but it will give you the self assurance you need to uncover these same types of tendencies as they relate to your other relationships. What you will find is that this evaluation will help build upon three critical aspects of our ultimate potential:

1. - Self-esteem – This is one of the most important human qualities. It's basically the belief that you really deserve to be a happy and successful person, combined with a deep and soulful trust in your own abilities.
2. - Self-image – How you feel about yourself is a critical piece of back nine success. We will talk more about this on hole #17 (Self Improvement), but the work you will do digging into your own family history and plans for the future will definitely help you in this regard.
3. - Self-confidence – This involves more than a belief that you can succeed. Self confidence has more to do with your belief that you can actually come back after you have failed, lost, or have been rejected.

As you build upon these three critical aspects of who you are, you will immediately gain more respect for yourself, and in turn, get more respect from others. One of the best ways to improve relationships is through respect. But as the old saying goes, in order to get respect, we must earn it. We must be respectable. This has been a huge wake-up call for me. As I look back upon most of my adult life, I didn't really have respect for myself. Even though I got respect from others in many facets of my life, I never really felt good about it due to the nature of my personal life, which was messy to say the least.

Health and Wellness (#11) – The basic premise here is that if you feel better and look better, you confidence will rise. As we just discussed, as your confidence rises, your ability to build solid relationships increases. As you improve your health and fitness, you put yourself in an excellent position to help others. How many people do you know who have a weight problem, health issues, etc..? How do these issues affect their lives? Helping people to find healthy solutions is probably the best way to improve relationships. This is so very important to me, as I feel that helping people is one of my true callings in life. When you actually set goals for yourself, and achieve them, you become a role model for others.

Knowledge (#12) – The more you know, the better you can communicate. Communication is the glue that holds all relationships together. In addition, when you make "learning" part of your life, you just have more to share. A good book, and good movie, music, TV shows, political insights, and sports updates. You name it, the more well-versed you are on a variety of topics, the most interesting you become. The more interesting you become the more others become interested in you. You see, relationship building works two ways. Giving and receiving. You can set yourself up for a much more interesting and enjoyable back nine as you increase your knowledge base.

Career (#13) – I was waiting for this one, this will be fun. This topic is very near and dear to me, because I have been building these types of relationships for over twenty years.

As I mentioned earlier, many of my business colleagues have become personal friends of mine. The reason for this is because I have worked tirelessly to make sure this happened. I am very proud of what I have been able to accomplish in this regard, and I consider it one of my greatest "front nine" achievements. If you remember from the career section, we spend one third of our lives at work. Therefore, many of our best relationships are going to come from our place of employment. The old adage "I don't mix business with personal" has gone out the window years ago. It works the opposite way as well for some people. I have always been very amused by the following statement when going out to dinner with business colleagues. "Let's not talk about business!" For me, talking about business, our families, the latest book we are reading, etc…are all open topics of conversation. This is how relationships are formed, and I have spent many years perfecting this craft. I know, that's a bit of an "ego-statement," but let me just roll with it for now.

Let me provide an example of what I am referring to when I talk about how our careers and relationship building go hand in hand. My last role in the wholesale mortgage space was, by far, the most incredible working experience I have had to date.

I was part of something really special a few years back, working for the largest financial institution in the world, yet for a division that was basically brand new. It was a blast, and I was able to build some fantastic and lasting relationships from this endeavor. In order to really grasp the impact of what I am referring to here, I am going to share an e-mail message with you that I sent to my colleges the day

I found out that the company was getting ready to shut our division down. Here's the message I sent:

"I could start this message by telling you that I really don't know what to say, but that wouldn't be truthful. I do know what to say, and it's a message that I hope will resonate with each of you. I have no books to draw from this time, nor do I have any clever quotes, analogies, or catch phrases to dazzle your senses. No inspiration from John Maxwell, Jeffery Fox, Jeffery Gitomer, Jim Collins, Dean Smith, Lou Holtz, Brian Lawrence, Jack Welch, Tony Dungy, Larry Bossidy, Tony Robbins, or Colin Powell. Just Tony Caico, a person who is humbled by this incredible experience and is very thankful for having played a critical role in this excellent journey. As many of you know, life has been quite difficult for me in 2008, and I am certainly not out of the woods yet. However, I can say unequivocally that this has absolutely been the most awesome experience of my entire business career. I can actually say that now, because my career has spanned sixteen years. WOW, I am getting old (not really...just getting started). Eleven of these business years have been in the mortgage industry, which is an industry under assault right now, but one that will endure, I am sure. I would like each of you to kick back for a minute and consider what we have accomplished together at CHE. We actually built a $16BB mortgage business from scratch with a very limited infrastructure. I am not sure what the record will state after this mess, but let me assure you, not many other organizations can say that, no matter where you look. Sure, we have had some loan losses, and yes, things have gone south recently, but NOBODY can ever take away what we have accomplished.

I, for one, am heading out the door with my head held high. I am very proud, and you should be to.

When I came on board in August of 2004, I inherited eight account executives on the East Coast, and we were booking about $30MM per month. I will always be thankful for this initial group of AEs (you know who you are) who helped me understand this business from day one. When I was first contacted about the position, I was hesitant. I figured out quickly that I had to get to $100MM per month of second mortgage business in a rather short period of time to meet my personal income targets. For some reason, it seemed to fit right away for me, and I had instant faith in our management team and what they were attempting to build. Still, the $100MM per month target seemed like a long way off. Fortunately, for me, I was able to surround myself with many more qualified individuals, and after only three months on the job, I exceeded that number, and increased the sales staff to forty. I never looked back, and at the peak of this endeavor in the east, I am very proud to say, that I was working with a group of mortgage professionals (you great folks) that funded over $580MM per month of second mortgage business...and finished the year at $6BB. In my book, these are awesome numbers and it was a phenomenal achievement. Something I will never forget. We had the people, we had the formula, and we "executed" beyond anyone's expectations.

This is the absolute truth....never let anyone tell you different...and NEVER forget it!!!!!

I will also never forget the two phenomenal national sales meetings (Vegas and AZ) and the two awesome Presidents Club events (Whistler and Palm Beach) that I was fortunate enough to attend during my tenure. The camaraderie displayed in Las Vegas in 2005 will have a lasting impact on me. Two of the proudest moments of my career have been the two opening cocktail receptions at our national sales meetings. These events had all of the things I enjoy. Business discussions, great friends, great beverages, and great conversations with an amazing group of people. For me, this is what it was (and still is) all about: adding value to someone's life, and having an opportunity for them to add value to mine. These were very special times for me, and I know my sentiment is shared by many of you reading this today. In addition, the speech that I heard from Lou Holtz in Palm Beach last year is another moment that is stitched on my brain, and I will draw upon that inspiration throughout my life. Being "significant" to as many people as I can is my true calling in life. Everything I have done, and everything I will do from here on out will be soaking in that premise. I sincerely hope that I left have each of you with something.

Whether it's been a series of conversations we had or just an e-mail or two, relationships have been the basis of my employment here at CHE. Although my e-mails have been a bit sparse in recent days (for obvious reasons) I have certainly tried my best to make each of you better. Please know, you have certainly made me a better manager and better person.

But, in the end, what I am most proud of is, YOU. ALL OF YOU. I have saved every e-mail that I have received regarding your appreciation of my monthly correspondence and the other things I have done for you. I remember ALL of the conversations and e-mails regarding how I was able to assist many you with your mindset during great times and not so great times. I have watched many of you grow in the last 4 years...and I am honored to have had the opportunity to spend time with each of you. You have inspired me...and I will call upon that inspiration as I ponder my next endeavor. I consider many of you, not only my business colleagues, but my dear friends. My only regret is that I didn't have more time spend with you, especially those of you that have come on board within the last year. Due to the industry changes, and the many variables in our business, my time has been spent on other items. I really didn't get to know you at all.

For me, the relationship piece has been the most rewarding, and these are things I will not forget.

The relationships that I have built, and the lasting friendships that I hope will endure. I sincerely wish you ALL great success, and would love to stay in touch with EACH AND EVERY one of you excellent people. Your friend...Tony"

This was my final letter to my colleagues and my team. I have saved every response that I received from this e-mail, and sometimes they bring me to tears. Just the fact that I remembered all of great times and individual nuances of these folks, and that I have touched so many of them fills me with a sense of joy that I can hardly describe. The message went out to over three hundred people, and I received feedback from over two hundred of them. Whenever I am feeling down, I refer to feedback from people that I have enlightened and inspired, and it always brings me back to center. You see, even though I was not fully living an authentic life back then, I was still attempting to "live" my true path. I am so thankful for that time and for all of the great relationships that were forged as a result.

Spirituality (#14) – We can not get through an entire chapter about relationships without talking about the relationship we have with our maker. Again, depending on your beliefs this could be described as your "one-true source." I love the way that sounds. I just got through listening to a book on tape by Dr. Wayne Dyer, entitled *Excuses Be Gone*. It was an awesome experience for me, and I learned quite a bit about myself and the reasons why I have been holding on to my "stuff" for too long. It's a very spiritual journey and experience about taking responsibility, letting go, moving forward, and staying "connected" with your one, true source. This for me is God. My relationship with God has always been there, but I certainly had lost focus on him over the years. I am just now working my way back to him, identifying with my faith, and doing my best to rebuild my relationship with God. On #12 you read about Rick Warren's *A Purpose Driven Life*, where he talks about developing your friendship with God. This has been a challenge for me, but I am trying hard and believe I am on the right path.

He goes on to say:

"You are as close to God as you choose to be. Like any friendship, you must work on your friendship with God. It won't happen by accident. It takes desire, time, and energy. If you want a deeper, more intimate connection with God you must learn to honestly share your feelings with him, trust him when he asks you to do something, learn to care about what he cares about, and desire his friendship more than anything else."

Yes, this is a challenge for many, especially for folks like me who are just now (at age forty five) realizing the magnitude of this relationship. There is another fantastic book that I recently read, entitled *The Shack,* by William Paul Young, that really helped me in this regard. I felt so moved by the main character's relationship with God throughout this book; I decided to write a book review and share my thoughts on this impactful piece of literature. Again, in true *My Back Nine* form, let me share what I wrote:

I just got finished reading one of the most incredible books I have ever read, and there is a force beyond my control that is typing these words right now. Heck, I don't even know what I am going to say, but I can assure you it will have deep meaning for me. I hope it will for you. The book is entitled The Shack, by William Paul Young, and it was recommended to me by two of my closest friends. Their recommendations were served up within days of each other, and their individual places in my life are separated my many years. The first is an old and dear friend of mine from college. This person has been such a valuable and supportive friend to me over the years. We met while I was a freshman in college and he was a senior. For some reason (sports, music, the college bar, girls, etc.), we took a liking to each other and I was introduced to all of his friends, who were also seniors. Typically, in college, seniors do not hang out with freshman (it's just not cool), but I never really did follow any conventional rules.

Anyway, I was in the group, and my first year at college was by far my most enjoyable, thanks to this group of friends I made. Most of whom I am still acquainted with, but this one person and I are still very close after 25 years or so. The other recommendation came from one my newest friends. She and I have started an excellent relationship, and she has made a tremendous impact on my life. She has been there for me throughout the absolute most difficult time of my life, and I am so grateful for her. She and I share so much in common with regard to personal growth, spirituality, and many other facets of life. So, there it is, two very special people (they know who they are) offering up a recommendation for a book, how could I go wrong?

Well, this book has touched me in ways I could not have imagined. A life changer, for sure. The timing of this read was perfect for me, as so much of the deep rooted meaning within these pages reflects upon many facets of life that I have been contemplating over the last few years. Mostly about God, spirituality, and the multitude of "unanswered" questions associated with this topic. In addition, I totally identified with the main character of this book. We have so much in common, it was like the book was written for me, a feeling that I am quite sure many others get when they ingest this book. Although they never quite gave his age, it seemed to me that he was in his mid-forties. He had five children, the youngest being a girl. He had some tragic things happen to him over the course of his life, and he could not bear to live with his pain. The similarities between this guy and me were haunting me throughout the book.

Did you ever hear the expression, "This book was so good, I couldn't put it down"? Well, I read this book in one day. Sure, I have done that before, but not with such passion and conviction.

I was literally lost in this guy's world for the entire time. I laughed, I cried (a bunch), and I re-read so many of the educational pieces about God and our relationship with him. It was a fascinating experience, one that I will not soon forget.

This book is fiction, which excited me from the beginning. I really have to force myself to read fiction, as I historically have more of an affinity for non-fiction. I'm looking right now at the back cover, and this quote sums it up:

"This story reads like a prayer – like the best kind of prayer, filled with sweat and wonder and transparency and surprise. If you read one fiction book this year, let this be it."

– Mike Morrell

I'll try not to give too much away, but the basic plot centers on a tragedy involving the main character's (Mack) youngest daughter. This alone through me over the edge on a few different chapters.

Both the tragedy and joy that flows around this little girl flung me into a waterfall of tears that were, at times, uncontrollable. My youngest child is also a little girl, so anyone who has children (especially a young daughter), I am warning you now, break out the tissues. The unspeakable horror of these events starts a long and painful journey for the main character, who ends up face to face with God himself. Or in this case, God herself...but that's all I am saying on that topic.

He receives an anonymous note, from whom he believes is God who wants to meet him in the exact location of the tragedy with his baby girl. He decides to take the journey, and he becomes witness to a wonder of events and experiences that will change his life forever. He gets to interact with God, ask questions, and face his demons and his past, and ultimately his darkest nightmare. What is so fantastic about this book is that the questions he asks are the same ones we all have: What is heaven like, and how can I get there? Where is God in a world so filled with unspeakable pain? Couldn't God have avoided what happened to his daughter—what happens to us? What about religion, which one is right? How do I know that God is with me?

Mack gets his answers relayed back to him with deep meaning and conviction. The dialog between Mack, God (as well as Jesus and the Holy Spirit) is captivating. The examples they use to explain the content are easily understood and transferable to our own lives and experiences. Again, I felt like someone was actually explaining all of these things to me. I was actually getting some of my own questions answered. What I realized is that God is always there, and that the circumstances of life are driven by our human desire to be independent. Yes, God knows what is going to happen, but that doesn't mean he will stop it from happening. God made us to love, to be humble, to be peaceful, and to live in his image. The image he clearly set for us when he sent his son, Jesus, to earth was to set the example. However, he also gave us all free will to make our own decisions, and many of us have taken advantage of this free will and to let the other dude (the one who resides a bit further south) have his way with us.

Certainly, that is what happened to me. What I now realize is that God has always been there for me. I realize that He is actually teaching me a great lesson throughout my recent struggles, and I have the opportunity for spiritual growth, forgiveness, and redemption, which is a lesson I am thankful for, and this book really brought it home for me. Regardless of your religious or spiritual views, you will LOVE this book. The statement underneath the title says: "Where tragedy meets eternity." One of the things I have learned from reading this book is that we can be in this world but don't have to be of this world. There is something greater waiting for us; all we have to do is believe

Leadership (#15) – We talked extensively about what it means to lead ourselves in life, and that regardless of the role we play, leadership is a critical component. Relationship building flows in direct proportion with our ability to lead the way. Remember, this is our back nine we are talking about, which is very important stuff. To keep people in our lives and to add people to our lives, we need to continue to develop our leadership qualities.

> ***Back on the course***. *That was a really good stroke on that putt; I can't believe it didn't go in. I know, you can't believe it, either. It seemed to me that almost the entire ball went in the cup, but then it rimmed out. Oh, well, it was a good stroke. Sometimes, you can hit a fantastic putt, but luck is just not on your side. That's OK; you are only left with a tap-in par...about three inches from the hole. Go ahead... knock it in!!!*

Stroke 4 – Romantic Relationships

Well, here we go. The five-thousand pound gorilla, for me anyway. I thought long and hard about whether or not I should add this piece. After much consideration, I figured that I would be remiss if I didn't at least make an attempt. After all, can I really talk in depth about relationships without broaching this topic? Can I really just leave out one of the most important topics regarding relationships? The answer is no, and I promise I will do my best.

In case you haven't figured this out by now, there is a reason why this shot is just a short "tap-in." I am a bit nervous about writing about this, because I have a long way to go when it comes to improving my ability to have a meaningful and sustainable romantic relationship. However, I am going to dive in anyway because I am quite sure that many back niners feel the same way. So, just like all of these other difficult shots, let's execute this one together. Like most back niners, I have had many romantic relationships throughout my life. Certainly

116

some were better than others, but never once have I had what I would refer to as a "perfect romantic relationship." As a matter of fact, over the years, I have questioned whether or not they really exist and whether or not two people are actually meant to stay together. I think differently now. I know they exist; I just wasn't capable of having one. This is my back nine, and your back nine. The time in our lives where we really take a close look at ourselves. The time in our lives where we examine what went wrong and what we are going do to fix it. I honestly believe that I was never "emotionally mature" enough to have an excellent relationship, mostly because throughout my entire adult male life, I was never really a whole person. I never developed my core, my center, and without that development, you can't possibly bring yourself into a great relationship.

In my view, a great romantic relationship only works one way. When two people are totally comfortable with themselves, and they each bring that comfort and confidence into a relationship that becomes fifty/fifty. I never felt the comfort or the confidence. Sure, on the surface, I seemed to have tremendous confidence.

I have never had great difficulty navigating with the opposite sex. Over the years, I am quite sure that I have charmed and fooled many, but never myself. I have always had quite an attraction to the opposite sex, and possessed many quality skills and maneuvers to aid in my conquests. But most of it was inauthentic, and deep down, I always knew. I usually didn't stay around long enough for the other person to figure it out. However, on the few occasions that I did, my lack of authenticity revealed itself in some manner and the relationship would end. That's OK, that's the past and I am sure everyone goes through similar trials on this topic. I am thankful now to know that I can change. I have changed, and I am on my way to becoming an entirely different person. An authentic person, who will be capable of true love, openness, honesty, and will be ready to share his entire self with someone at some point and time. That actually felt really good. I am not going to spend time talking about prior relationships. You can quickly ascertain from what you have already read that I wasn't really successful in this department. I am also not going to spend much time on the negatives, because most of the negative aspects that caused me to have strained romantic relationships have faded, or are at least in the process of going away. For example, having a huge ego, being extremely demanding, having unrealistic expectations, expecting sex all of the time, lacking respect, and being in control kind of sum up the negatives. No wonder I had difficulty here. However, I think it's better to focus on the positives, the things I know I do well, and the things I know I need to improve upon. I hope as you read through these lines, you will draw upon your own strengths and weaknesses when it comes to romantic relationships. For me, I have always been generous, affectionate, communicative, supportive, and romantic. Some of my new traits which will hopefully lead towards love are being humble, attentive, helpful, respectful, and loving. I also take good care of myself, love to go shopping, get manicures and pedicures, spa treatments, enjoy pop music, enjoy chick flicks, and many other things most men despise. I see this as an advantage for me, because I truly enjoy these things. It's not a game for me anymore, and I am hopeful these qualities will help me find that elusive "soul-mate" that everyone searches for. No, this is not a Match.com add, just trying to communicate that I have made much progress. Something that I hope many of you can draw upon as you attempt to improve your chances for LOVE on your back nine.

Back on the course. Tap-in par...well done. It was a little more challenging than you thought, certainly it was for me, but we made it through and got our par. On to 17!!!

#17 – "What Are You Doing To Improve Your Golf Game?" - Par 4

"That man is a success who has lived well, laughed often and loved much; who has gained the respect of intelligent men and the love of children; who has filled his niche and accomplished his task; who leaves the world better than he found it, whether by an improved poppy, a perfect poem, or a rescued soul; who never lacked appreciation of earth's beauty or failed to express it; who looked for the best in others and gave the best he had."

— Robert Louis Stevenson

"To laugh often and much, to win respect of intelligent people and the affection of children; to earn the appreciation of honest critics and endure betrayal of false friends; to appreciate beauty, to find the best in others, to leave the world a bit better, whether by a healthy child, a garden patch or a redeemed social condition; to know even one life has breathed easier because you have lived. This is to have succeeded"

—Ralph Waldo Emerson

On the course *– OK, you guys ready for this one? Number seventeen is very difficult. It's the longest par 4 on the entire golf course, measuring 450 yards. This is par 5 distance for* *most amateurs, but something tells me that you are totally ready for this hole. Your preparation and focus has been stellar throughout this back nine, and this will come in handy as you make your way through 17. The tee shot needs to be long and straight, as trees line both sides of the fairway. In addition, there is a water hazard on the right side, just beyond the tress, about 230 yards out. The water continues all the way up the right side to a peninsula green. It's a dog leg right, but you need to be sure you keep your ball on the left side. If you try and skirt the trees with your drive, you will bring the hazard into play. The shot from the left side is a longer, but safer play. Of course, as in most golf holes, an excellent drive straight down the middle will do just fine. Your approach shot will require the same accuracy as your drive, in an attempt to avoid the water hazard on the right and the sand bunker on the left. It's OK, you have been preparing for this hole all day, and you are ready. Steady your nerves, clear your head, and stripe it down the middle!!*

Stroke 1 - Personal Growth/Self Improvement

Before I begin this shot by outlining why I chose personal growth as one of the nine most important aspects of our lives, let me explain why I have two quotes to start this hole on self improvement. Obviously, as you can see by now, I am a huge fan of inspiration quotes. They are peppered throughout this book, as I attempt to serve up a correlation between the topic and the quote. I feel that it is sometimes easier to remember a small quote that reminds us of some deeper meaning in our lives. I have many books on quotes, daily devotionals, and other reading materials that I review quite often in search of a great quote. Sometimes they provide me with inspiration to write a blog, and sometimes it just helps me get through my day with more focus and discipline. Either way, it has become a personal "quest" for me and has added tremendous value to my life. On some of the golf holes we have played, I just couldn't seem to find the right quote. So, I created the quote myself, a bit of "tongue and cheek" humor on the surface, but a deep meaningful expression of what I truly wanted to convey underneath. Unlike some of the other golf holes where I couldn't exactly find what I was looking for, #17 was different as I actually found two quotes that I felt pertinent to the message.

Both quotes by Robert Louis Stevenson and Ralph Waldo Emerson (I love those names) are hauntingly similar. So much so, that I thought that maybe one read the other's quote and tried to say it better. After conducting some research on these two great writers, it's difficult to ascertain whose quote came first, although Emerson was born about twenty years before Stevenson. They were both prominent literary figures during the same time in history (1800s). Robert Louis Stevenson was from Scotland and Ralph Waldo Emerson was an American, so maybe they had some sort of competition between them. Either way, these quotes are perfect as the authors identify vividly with their views on what it means to be successful. In both descriptions, they let us know that a journey without continued personal growth will never lead us down the path to personal success.

OK, let's get going on to the subject matter at hand, Self-Improvement. It seems to me that we have sort of come full circle, and we have come right back to where we started.

I love the way all of theses components tie together, but this one, #17, will actually prove to be the blood that flows through our back nine veins as we set out to improve all aspects of our lives. This all-important and critical component is really what this entire project is all about. Like the quotes state above, we all want respect, we all want love, we all want affection, we all want to fulfill our task or mission, we all want to see the best in others, we all want to give our best, and ultimately be our best. We have talked much about adding all of the aspects of the nine components into our daily lives. We started off in our introduction (or the turn) attempting to analyze all of the things that have gone wrong in the first half of our lives. We may have thought that we were always trying to improve ourselves, but somehow, somewhere, things started falling through the cracks. Somehow, life just got in the way. We went to school, started careers, started families, and many of us (certainly me) just stopped working on our own personal improvements. Many of us took the wrong path, and we ended up, right here, right now, searching for something that will help us get our lives back on track. So, what do we do? How do we improve? Well, here's the good news, we are doing it, right now.

You have picked up this book and you have played these important golf holes right beside me. We have analyzed, together, so many important aspects of our lives, and now it's time to put them into play. Now, it's time to make each of these components a daily part of our lives. Now is the time to take a hard stance on YOU, and to put a detailed game plan together that will ensure that your back nine will be as fabulous as it ought to be. We ALL deserve the elusive "happiness" that has been missing from our lives, something we will talk more about on #18. But improving our lives each day, while we embark upon this back nine journey, well, that is what our endeavor is all about.

I received an e-mail from a friend last year, entitled 2009. It was basically a list of forty items (I condensed it to **32**...*there's that number again*) that we should be focused on throughout our days in order to improve our lives in the coming year. This list provides a solid framework for daily improvement, and it's an excellent way for me to illustrate the importance of continued self improvement. As you read through the following items, try and take some notes on where you stand with each one of these items. This was an eye opening exercise for me. My first attempt was in December 2008, which is when I received the e-mail. I put a check mark next to the statements that I had already incorporated into my life, and left the others blank. I only checked the items off that I "really" believed I was doing and/or living.

Well, I checked off twenty one of the **32** in December, and I am pleased to say that I just did it again (six months later), and check off twenty eight of **32**. I was very satisfied with my recent results, because it shows me that I am living more authentically and really "practicing what I am preaching." Anyway, I copied and pasted it to my back nine file, and somehow knew that it would come in handy somewhere during my writing. I have actually changed many of these around and added some "back nine flavor" to each in an attempt to inspire myself along the way. I now have them taped to my wall in my office, and look at them daily. Here we go:

1. Take a ten to thirty minute walk every day. And while you walk, smile. It is the ultimate anti-depressant. I usually listen to my iPod, which has all of my favorite songs. This helps me keep the smile on my face. Remember what smiling does for our overall health? (See #11)

2. When you wake up in the morning complete the following statement, "My purpose is to _____ today." I do this on my calendar, and fill out in the blank space I created every day.

3. Live with the three E's -- Energy, Enthusiasm, and Empathy. These are great words, but you get very creative here, and choose your own words. I usually change my words each month. For example, this month they are Faith, Focus, and Family.

4. Play more games and read more books than you did in 2008. I really can't get my hands on enough reading material. Something we discussed in detail in on #12 (knowledge). My kids and I love playing board games; Monopoly and Scrabble seem to be the games of choice right now. We played Monopoly last night, and my six year old won, fair and square, with no help from anyone.

5. Make time to practice meditation and prayer. They provide us with daily fuel for our busy lives. Read *The Bible* and *Illuminata (*by Marianne Williamson)

6. Spend time with people over the age of seventy and under the age of six. Appreciate their genuine nature, strength, and innocence. For real! This is easy for me, due to my family situation, but if you do not have this advantage, seek out children and elderly people to interact with. You can learn a great deal from have conversations with Senior Citizens, or *Master Citizens,* as I like to call them.

7. Dream more while you are awake. Read John Maxwell's book, *Put Your Dreams to the Test.*

8. Eat more foods that grow on trees and plants. Eat less food that is manufactured.

9. Drink green tea and plenty of water. Eat blueberries, wild Alaskan Salmon, broccoli, almonds and walnuts, dark chocolate and red wine.

10. Try to make at least three people smile each day. This is easier when you are smiling yourself.

11. Clear clutter from your house, your car, your desk and let new and flowing energy into your life. This is very helpful. Having a clean and uncluttered space around you helps you focus on more important things and reduces your stress levels.

12. Don't waste your precious energy on gossip, issues of the past, negative thoughts or things you cannot control. Instead invest your energy in the positive present moment.

13. Realize that life is a school and you are here to learn. Problems are simply part of the curriculum that appear and fade away like algebra class, but the lessons you learn will last a lifetime.

14. Eat breakfast like a king, lunch like a prince, and dinner like a college kid.

15. Life isn't fair, but it's still good. Get over it and try and separate yourself from your circumstances. Read *The Power of Now* (Eckart Tolle) and *The Shack* (William Paul Young).

16. Life is too short to waste time hating anyone. Forgive everyone for everything. Read *Excuses Be Gone* by Dr Wayne Dyer.

17. Don't take yourself so seriously. No one else does. Smiling, staying peaceful, and separating yourself from your circumstances will help you in this regard.

18. You don't have to win every argument. Agree to disagree. This is a difficult one from Type A personalities (like me). I historically always had to be right and prove my point. It's truly exhilarating to let this go. Trust me, I have done it…and it feels great.

19. Make peace with your past so it won't spoil the present. You will have limited back nine success if you do not incorporate this into your life.
20. Don't compare your life to others. You have no idea what their journey is all about. Keep your focus on yourself, your thoughts, and let go of expectations of what others will do or say.
21. No one is in charge of your happiness except you.
22. Frame every so-called disaster with these words: In five years, will any of this matter? This will help you move past the "little things in life" that people get stressed about but shouldn't.
23. What other people think of you is none of your business.
24. However good or bad a situation is it will change. Again, detaching your self from your experiences and circumstances will help you live in the present and enjoy each moment.
25. Your job won't take care of you when you are sick. Your friends will. Stay in touch.
26. Envy is a waste of time. You already have all you need. Practice being grateful each day. Wear something that will help keep you focused on what's important. I just designed and ordered "*My Back Nine*" rubber bracelets that I wear everyday as a reminder to stay the course.
27. No matter how you feel; get up, dress up, and show up. When you are feeling blue, get out of the house, get around people, and just DO and BE. What you will find is that your problems go away when your mind is occupied.
28. Do the right thing! We ALL know what this means.
29. Call your family often. These are the people that care about you the most, even if they don't show it at times. Do your part, and release the expectations. You will be both surprised and amazed with the results.
30. Each night before you go to bed complete the following statements: I am thankful for _____. Today I accomplished _____.

31. Remember that you are too blessed to be stressed. The best is yet to come!!
32. Enjoy the ride. Remember this is not Disney World and you certainly don't want a fast pass. You only have one ride through life so make the most of it and enjoy the ride.

"May your troubles be less, may your blessings be more, may nothing but happiness come through your door!"

– Author Unknown

Remember this number **"32"**. We will revisit it again on the 19th hole (conclusion) of the back nine.

Back on the course. *Well, this hole is about improvements, so it's no surprise to me that your tee shot is, again, lying in the middle of the fairway. You are playing a stellar and steady round of golf, and you have improved greatly throughout your back nine. Your tee shot was about 250 yards in length, so you are left with a fairly long approach into this peninsula green. Your have about 200 yards left, so be sure to make the proper club selection. This is a very difficult shot, but you are striking the ball like a pro, so it shouldn't be a problem. Keep your back straight, your left elbow close to your body, and put a smooth stroke on it!*

Stroke 2 – Adversity and Perseverance – Opportunities in Disguise

As we travel through this back nine and make plans for our future, we can be sure that we will continue to face obstacles along the way. Therefore, we will need to include some new strategies and tools to overcoming the objections that we are sure to face. Historically, I have not had much success overcoming objections. It's funny, though, because many things that happened to me didn't really affect me that much. It was always very easy for me to just brush it off, bury it away somewhere, and move on to something new. That was a mistake. A mistake that I have paid dearly for over the last several years. You see, we can't just tuck our problems away and never confront them. It all becomes part of our lives, and you can rest assured these hidden gems will rise up again and bite you when you least expect it. So, now that we are sure that we will face certain adversity, what do we to ensure that we are equipped to handle things better on the back nine? As you probably can ascertain from reading this book, I spend a lot of time learning from others. Usually through books that I read, but also through people that I know and dialog that we share. As and example, take a gander at this incredible chronology of adversity faced by one of the greatest Presidents in U.S. history:

- Failed in business in 1831
- Defeated for Legislature in 1832
- Second failure in business in 1833
- Suffered nervous breakdown in 1836
- Defeated for Speaker in 1838
- Defeated for Elector in 1840
- Defeated for Congress in 1843
- Defeated for Congress in 1848
- Defeated for Senate in 1855
- Defeated for Vice President in 1856
- Defeated for Senate in 1858
- Elected President in 1860

Wow, that is thirty years of adversity. Talk about perseverance. As I am sure you have all figured out, this was Abraham Lincoln. This man knew what he wanted, he identified with his path and his purpose (something we talked about in our Spirituality chapter), and he stayed the course. Check out his quote when Lincoln was asked about overcoming objections:

"Having chosen our course, without guile and with pure purpose, let us renew our trust in God, and go forward without fear and with manly hearts."

If that doesn't get your blood pumping for self improvement, you may need to check your pulse. I can tell you that when I am faced with adversity these days (which happens quite often); stories like this keep me going. I realize that every man and woman has adversity and everyone has a burden that seems unbearable at times. However, once you realize that it is part of life, and you equip yourself with more and more stories of perseverance and other tools, what you will find is that you too can overcome. Some of life's greatest achievements come through adversity. Many of the world's greatest achievements and inventions were accidents, or opportunities in disguise. The main reason that they proved to be so valuable was due to the fact that these folks never gave up. When I think of adversity, I sometimes go back to my childhood and think of a toy that I had. It was a Superman blow-up doll, with sand on the bottom, sort of like a punching bag. You remember those, right? It was my favorite toy, and each of my siblings had one, too, so we had many dolls to beat around the house. I would hit that Superman a hundred times, and a hundred times he would bounce back up. Eventually, I would throw him across the room, and guess what, he would still bounce back and stand up. That is what perseverance is all about, and I think about that Superman doll sometimes when I am really down and need to bounce back up.

The Superman punch doll is sort of like the story of Ernest Hemingway. This one is near and dear to me, since I have always been a huge fan of this great writer whom I aspire to be like. At one point and time early in his writing career, Hemmingway lost all of his manuscripts. His good friend and world renowned poet, Ezra Pound told him not to worry. He informed Hemmingway that this was a blessing (or opportunity) in disguise, because when he went to re-write what he has already written, Hemmingway would only remember the good parts and not the bad parts. The rest, they say, is History.

Adversity has been such a huge part of my life in the last few years, I have had to force myself to face many demons and deal with these challenges head-on. The book you are reading, right now, was given birth through adversity. Like I have said, this project started out as my own personal healing mechanism, and has just taken on a life of its own. My desire and ability to write has taken on new meaning in my life through adversity. In my view, your entire life is a series of tests, and your ability to take the tests, learn from the tests, and ultimately, overcome the obstacles your faced with when tested are key indicators of what type of back nine success you will achieve.

How about you? What is your test? What adversity are you going through? I know it's something. How are you handling your adversity? We should keep reminding ourselves that our time on this earth is brief, and our problems although insurmountable at times are all problems we can handle. Ultimately, it was all supposed to happen just the way it happened. Which path will you take in reaction to adversity?

> ***Back on the course.*** *That was an incredible shot, my friends. A four iron from two hundred yards out, with water all around, and your shot has landed softly on the green about twenty feet from the flagstick. You have hit many fine shots today, but that was truly remarkable. You have an excellent chance at birdie here, so stay calm and steady. This putt is fairly flat, but breaks left to right, about two feet or so. Go ahead, put a solid stroke on it and let it happen!!*

Stroke 3 – Improve your golf game, improve your life

I am hopeful that by now you are getting really excited about the endless possibilities for improvements on your back nine. We have already identified so many areas of our lives that we can improve upon, and we still have a few more to discuss. I am also hopeful that each and every one of you will embrace your "kaizen," which is *a commitment to continuous improvement.*

This is awesome and powerful stuff, and our momentum is building. We are starting to tap into the power that lies within each of us to move forward, to improve, to make a difference, and to advance ourselves and the people in our lives. However, in order to truly make the necessary changes in our lives, we still have some examining to do. We still need to identify with some of the things that have been holding us back and causing strain in our lives. In order to uncover some of these items, I feel that this is a great time to draw upon some comparisons between golf and life. Throughout our journey, we have gone back to the course after each shot. However, on this stroke, we are actually going to dissect our golf game, our golf swing (with respect to our lives), and determine what we need to do to improve. Let's just say we are going to take a break and go to the practice range for a while. Not typical in the middle of the round, but what the heck, this is our back nine and we can do what we please.

If you recall, in the introduction, I talked about my own golf game, and how the bad habits I had developed on the golf course were quite similar to some of the bad habits I had developed in my life. Poor planning, poor preparation, impatience, anger, frustration, and inauthenticity were just some of the characteristics that were consistent in my golf game and in my life. If I (we) are going to really improve on our back nine, we will need to make sure that we understand exactly where these deficiencies came from, and develop some strategies to make sure they leave us for good. We have done some of this work already, but let's put the finishing touches on now.

Let me start off by referring to a short golf story that shows up in the first chapter of Deepak Chopra's book, *Golf for Enlightenment*. This will give us a great starting point to tackle this shot, and help us uncover some deficiencies of our own in an attempt to build upon our self improvement skills. The main character is this book (Adam) is about to go on an unexpected journey. He basically starts out like a typical frustrated middle-aged golfer (sound familiar?) and ends up with a sense of presence, hope, and enlightenment for his golf game and ultimately his life. Which is exactly what we are attempting to accomplish on our back nine, right?

OK, here we go:

"Adam had just made a horrible tee shot – a low, limping hook that wound up in the rough. He blinked in disbelief. The ball had barely made it eighty yards. But then everything had been going badly. His body was full of tension from past disasters. After he went bogey, bogey, double bogey on the sixth, seventh, and eighth holes, Adam's partners had stopped saying "It's only a game." They talked about the stock market and moved on. Adam was so angry he didn't even set up his next shot and ended up whiffing it. Without

pausing, he hacked at it again. A second whiff. This time his shoulders whirled around so fast that he almost toppled over. Adam felt the blood rush to his face. He was sure he could hear muffled guffaws from the foursome behind. They were waiting on the tee, watching him make a fool of himself eighty yards out. His own group, feeling pellets of rain, had rushed ahead to the green. "Stand back, take a look, give it one practice swing, than fire," Adam murmured, repeating the ritual drilled into him by his coach.

His next attempt, a choppy savage swipe, cut a half-moon into the cover of the ball. It jumped up like a wounded duck and flew straight across the fairway into the opposite rough. "Lying four," one of the spectators shouted from the tee.
Only one thing was on Adam's mind at that moment, and it wasn't this cruel endeavor they called a game: He only begged fate to get everybody's eyes off him. So he trotted across the fairway, snatched a lofted club, and stared the ball down again. It grinned up at him with its new crooked smile. "This time I am going to kill you," he promised. Whack! It took a safari to find the shot, which went a long way but veered wickedly right. Adam's caddy was up for it. A new kid, he was getting far too much entertainment value out of this round. "It's a terrible lie. Want me to show you?" he said helpfully, pointing to the woods. "Not if you want to live," Adam muttered between his gritted teeth. He went in alone with a wedge, hacking at the dead brush. Spider webs clung to his sweating face. Something low to the ground slithered away. Now it was coming down to survival. He got to his ball, which was half-buried in mud and slimy leaves. Gray drizzle was filtering through the pines, gathering in big cold drops that plucked on the back of Adam's neck. He was past hating the rude onlookers, the treacherous hazards, the dismal weather, his bad luck, his awful swing, and even himself. He couldn't remember feeling more alone.

If you are like me, you have experienced very similar circumstances on the golf course. As we draw some comparison to our lives and our "front nine" experiences, this little episode reminds us of how our attitudes, lack of preparation, and basic demeanor could have been the cause for some of our bad behaviors and some of our poor decisions. That's OK, because we have now taken a close look at our history, our family situations, our spirituality, our learning ability, our health, our careers, our leadership qualities, and our relationships. Our focus on these topics will prepare us for a future that will be clear of the same mistakes. We will learn to take new paths, the less traveled paths that we always knew were the right paths; we were just too afraid to take them. We will learn to develop different kinds of memory, one that includes a short-term memory for failure and a long-term memory for success.

In Bob Rotella's *Golf Is Not a Game of Perfect*, he draws upon a unique comparison between Mark Twain and Fred Couples (another personal favorite). You noticed above that Adam's anger was out of control, something that happens all too often on the golf course. I can speak from personal experiences. My anger was so bad at times, that many of my close friends really didn't enjoy playing with me. I would get so wrapped up in my inability to score, a missed putt, a shot out of bounds, etc…that I could barely function. I remember feeling my heart beat elevate, and getting so emotional and angry, I would swear I would never play again. I would barely talk with anyone when I was playing poorly, something that happened quite often, solely due to my attitude and my inability to forget bad shots. Similar to Adam's experience above, most of our anger on the golf course comes from being unable to forget the bad shots. The anger of the bad shots and poor performance stays so firmly planted and ingrained in our memory, the unfocused golfer gets little joy or satisfaction even from a good shot that follows. All of this ultimately leads to more frustration, a consistent bad attitude, and even worse golf scores. Mark Twain, who wasn't even known to be a golfer, said it best:

"The inability to forget is infinitely more devastating than the inability to remember."

If you think about this carefully, you will find that this scenario works the same way in life. Many of us have such a hard time forgiving ourselves for a mistake; we just never let it go. It just continues to fester and build up inside of us, until it manifests itself into another mistake and/or bad decision. The key here is to adjust our thinking by filling our minds with happy thoughts, memories, and positive outcomes.

These are the things we need to draw upon when faced with adversity. We will all face adversity, for sure. The question is which shot will we remember, the good shot or the bad shot. As an example, Bob Rotella had dinner with Fred Couples, the night before he won the 1992 Masters. Fred asked Bob, who is a physiological coach for sport professionals, what he thought about his mental game. Bob, having never worked with Fred before said he didn't know, but asked Fred what he thinks about. He said the following:

"Well, you know, when I come up to a shot, I just pull up my sleeves and shrug my shoulders to try and get relaxed. And then I try and remember the best shot I ever hit in my life with whatever club I have in my hand. Is that OK?"

This is awesome, and a perfect illustration of projecting a positive mental attitude before embarking upon a challenge. Sounds like Fred Couples had read and understood Mark Twain's quote above. Whether it's a golf game, a work situation, or a family decision, this one "swing thought" will help you in tight situations.

Let's stay out on the practice range for just another moment or two, as we continue to find ways to improve by drawing references to this fabulous game of golf.

In Darren Gee's book, *The Seven Principles of Golf,* he helps us identify the synergy between how to improve your golf game and how to improve your life. Let me go through his seven principles, with some added *back nine flavor* from my own experiences, to show you what I mean:

The First Principle – Get grounded (*quiet your mind, ground your body, find your center*) – This first principle has been the single most important change that I have made in my life and in my golf game.

I find that I have developed better listening skills, and that I don't always have to be right. I have always had a calm exterior, but my now I am developing an equally calm and focused interior to match. Reading two books by Eckart Tolle has really helped me in this regard. Both *The Power of Now* and *A New Earth* are great reference books on finding your center, staying present, keeping your mind quiet and separating yourself from your circumstances.

The Second Principle – Develop Feel (*slow down and notice, make the connection, do what feels right*) - Our lives get really hectic at times, and we seem to have a hard time slowing down. In life and golf, we really need to slow down if we wish to connect with our source. As humans, we have an uncanny ability for developing feelings, but we sometimes have difficulty deciphering the good feelings from the bad. In the end, we know what feels right and we know what feels wrong.

Our challenge is to stay on the right course, and not give in to temptations that will cause us harm in the future.

The Third Principle – Visualize the Shot (*know what you want, believe in what you want, see it happen*) - As in the example with Fred Couples above, it's important that we visualize the things we want to come true in our lives. In the Spirituality chapter, I talked about my "vision board" and how it helps me stay targeted on what I want to have happen in the future. Be careful here, though, because thinking about the future too much will deter to you from living today, and staying in the present. Visualize will help you perform today, and the rest will take care of itself.

The Fourth Principle – Create Your Own Pre-shot Ritual (*create a personal ritual, find your own space, honor your ritual daily*) - Before we hit each shot in golf, we must perform the same routine. This helps us stay in rhythm and helps us to not have to remember every little detail of our golf swing. Life is no different. Develop better schedules and routines for your days. Keep journals, calendars, and constant reminders of what you need to be doing. This is a very individual process, so do not look at someone else's schedule to determine what you should be doing. Create your own space, and write down what that looks like for you. What you will find is that you will create the space that you were always meant to be in. You will want to have these processes written out, and over time, these processes and rituals will seem like second nature. Then, you will be in your comfort zone, a place that is safe and warm, and a place that you can continue to grow. The preparation for this phase is key. If it's done half-way and you are not consistent, you will stall your growth and hamper your ability to improve.

The Fifth Principle – Find Your Natural Swing (*trust your instincts, find your own way, search your soul*) – Trusting your instincts is a tricky one. I spent most of my adult male life trusting my instincts, but some of those instincts led me down the wrong path. What I now know is that some of those instincts lacked authenticity. They were instincts that came from trying to impress people, trying to keep up with others, and were solely based in an ego state. I wasn't true to myself, and therefore unable to find my own way. Now that I have searched my soul and uncovered my true spirit, I am on my way and plowing the fields through my true and authentic path. So, go ahead and trust your instincts, but only after you have found your way.

The Sixth Principle – Play One Shot at a Time (*turn off the autopilot, be present now, surrender to the moment*) - Again, *The Power of Now* is my best suggestion to help you stay in the present and surrender to each moment. This book was a life changer for me, as I learned a whole different set of skills to help me in my journey. Break up your routines; it's truly the only way to live fully in the moment. Let go of some of those bad habits that have hampered your growth and performance. Let go of the pain that you have been holding onto and commit to change.

The Seventh Principle – Transform Your Golf Game, Transform Your Life (*trust the process, embrace the journey, transform your life*) - When I play golf now I truly enjoy myself. I was playing several months back with a dear friend of mine who has been playing with me for 25 years. He told me that he had never had more fun playing with me than he had that weekend. He said I was just different, and it seemed like I was totally separated from the outcome of each shot and each hole. I didn't score so well, because my short game was out of practice, but I hit the ball better than I ever have, and really learned a lot about myself in the process. This is a process that I now trust, both in golf and in my life. I really do embrace every day like it's my last, and my life has definitely changed. I am hopeful that yours will too.

I will conclude this chapter on self improvement with another piece of literature that hangs on the wall in my office. It's from *The Secret Scrolls*, by Rhonda Bird, and it's called, I *Promise Myself:*

"To be so strong that nothing can disturb my peace of mind. To talk health, happiness, and prosperity to every person I meet. To make all my friends feel that there is something worthwhile in them. To look at the sunny side of everything and make my optimism come true. To think only of the best, to work for only the best, and to expect the best. To be just as enthusiastic about the success of others as I am about my own. To forget the mistakes of the past and press on to the greater achievements of the future. To wear a cheerful expression at all times and give a smile to every living creature I meet. To give so much time to improving myself that I have no time to criticize others. To be too large for worry, too noble for anger, too strong for fear, and too happy to permit the presence of trouble. To think well of myself and to proclaim this fact to the world, not in loud words, but in great deeds. To live in the faith that the whole world is on my side, so long as I am true to the best that is in me."

— Christian D Larson

Back on the course. *Another birdie, what a great putt. Your putting stroke is so pure right now; you must feel like you can make everything. What a great hole you just played. An awesome tee shot, your "shot of the day" on your approach, and a solid twenty foot birdie putt right in the jar. Well done.... indeed. You are three under par with one hole to play. That's right, only one hole left, #18. Let's do it!!*

#18 – "Hole in One"- Par 3

"*The happiness which brings enduring worth to life is not the superficial happiness that is dependent on circumstances. It is the happiness and contentment that fills the soul even in the midst of the most distressing of circumstances and most bitter environment. It is the kind of happiness that grins when things go wrong and smiles through the tears. The happiness for which our souls ache is one undisturbed by success or failure, one which will root deeply inside us and give inward relaxation, peace, and contentment, no matter what the surface problems may be. That kind of happiness stands in need of no outward stimulus.*"

—Billy Graham

On the course – *Our last hole, #18, is a fairly short par 3, about 165 yards in length. There is no real danger on this hole. It is downhill, so it will play actually a bit shorter than 165 yards, depending on the wind direction. Today, the winds are calm, so you should be licking your chops to play this last hole. You have had quite a performance on this **back nine**, and all you have left is this short, downhill par 3 to play. After all of your hard work, you deserve to finish your round with this hole. The sky is Carolina Blue, and the scenery around this hole is spectacular.*

Take a deep breath, keep your head steady, and swing away!!

Stroke 1 – Happiness/Enlightenment

Well, my friends, we have reached the 18th hole. It's been quite a journey thus far, and now we get to tackle to "elusive" topic of Happiness. Some folks may prefer to use the word "enlightenment" to describe this life component. For me, they are sort of one in the same.

Not sure about any of you, but I have personally never experienced the "joy" of a hole in one, but I can imagine how it feels. I have hit shots in the hole from the fairway before for a few eagles, but never off the tee. One time I recall, years ago, I was playing on a TPC course in Sarasota, FL (*Prestancia*), and I hit a shot in the hole off the fairway for an eagle on #9. I can remember it vividly, because I was playing with my ex-wife's boss. We had tied the first eight holes, and I won all of the holes, the money, and the match on that one shot, which added to my excitement. I can remember hitting it as pure as I could and watching it go towards the whole. I can remember saying, "go in" which we all do from time to time, but it rarely does. Well, this time it did. The ball hit about ten feet in front of the hole, landed softly, and just rolled right into the hole. I put my arms up in the air and fell right down on my back. There was nobody watching, except my playing partner, of course, but it was pure ecstasy. I'm sure that you have all had moments like that. Moments of pure joy that sprung out of nowhere. Well, that is not entirely true. Some moments of joy come as a result of hard work, preparation, and dedication. Even my eagle, although extremely lucky, certainly had some measure of preparation and skill behind it. That's what we are searching for on this last hole so we can prepare ourselves and set ourselves up for those moments of joy and happiness. We all want to have these moments more often; we just don't know how to get them.

Let's begin with a definition:

Happiness is a state of mind or feeling such as contentment, satisfaction, pleasure, or joy.

This is perfect and exactly what we are going after. I am not going to go into a philosophical discussion on what happiness means to different people. What we will do is break down some of the elusive components of happiness and uncover some of the secrets to happiness that may have eluded us over the years.

This is one of our ultimate "goals" in life, and for some of us, the most important aspect of our lives. Regardless of where your *Happiness Meter* lies, let's face it; we ALL want to feel happy. We ALL want to feel contentment, satisfaction, pleasure, and joy. That's what we are after here, which is why this is our last and final hole. After all, why would we work so hard on all of these other aspects of our lives, if we can't experience the joy of our achievements, and the satisfaction of accomplishing our goals?

I have some more good news for you. What you will discover by playing this hole is that the work that we have already done on holes ten through seventeen will help us uncover some key points regarding happiness. To illustrate my point, I would like to share with you my *Twelve Secrets of Happiness.* As you read through this next section, try and draw some comparisons to your life, and see where you stand on each item. What you may find is that we have covered many of these items already, through our discussion the other eight components. You see, like I have been saying all along, it ALL ties together.

Optimism – The general feeling that something good will inevitably come out of all circumstances, even the very painful ones. Optimism helps minimize fears about the future that could otherwise become debilitating. To become a more "glass half-full" thinker takes hard work and focus, and is very difficult for many people, including me. Optimism is mostly about your attitude. In fact, the two words can be interchangeable at times. Attitude is a way of life and it contains your experiences, your environment, your opportunities, your problems, your choices, and your responses. Your attitude can become either the bolt that locks the door or the key that unlocks that same door. Which will it be for you?

Love – We have mentioned "love" a few times already on our back nine, but the sense of compassion for the people in your life and the feeling of knowing that you are cared for in return can be one of the biggest predictors of happiness. Whether it's romantic love, family love, or parental love, this is the best feeling in the world and truly enhances the overall satisfaction of our lives. There are three Greek words for love. They are: *agape, eros,* and *phileo. Eros* love refers to sensual love, *phileo* refers to brotherly love, and *agape* refers to selfless and giving love. It describes love as an act of will or a choice we make. It seems to me that all three are important in life, but **agape love** is most closely connected to our ultimate happiness.

Courage – Do you sometimes behave contrary to what you believe? How does that make you feel? Courage is standing up for what's important to you and keeping in line with your sense of right and wrong. If you don't, you will rob yourself of happiness and give in to self doubt. I have personal experience with this facet of happiness. My self doubt was directly attributed to my poor decisions and my actions quite often conflicted with my sense of right and wrong. How about you? Have you ever felt this way? To find true happiness, we must stay true to ourselves, without compromise and without fail.

Sense of Choice – People who describe themselves as "self-governing" or more likely to have satisfaction and happiness in their lives. This includes life balance, a practice where many of us fall short. Enjoying a better balance between work and the rest of your life, for example, can become another happiness thief. The good news here is that there is a powerful synergy between life balance and the contents of what you are reading in *My Back Nine*. If we stay focused on these nine key components of life, we are sure to find better balance and more happiness in our lives.

Proactive – Typically, the happiest people always seem to be on the prowl for new and exciting opportunities. They have a natural zest for life, and always seem to be moving forward. These folks are not afraid to make mistakes, and actually thrive on learning from them. There is scientific proof that diving into new experiences actually increases the production of Dopamine, one of the body's feel-good chemicals. Staying active and passionate about everything, even the small things in life, will raise your happiness meter for sure.

Security – Feeling good about your place in life. That is security. Happy people simply like who they are, and don't need to change to suit someone else's views or opinions. Even when things do not seem to be going your way, it may be helpful to have some sort of go-to mechanism in place to bring you back to center. For me, it's reading some of the e-mails and recommendations from people who lives I have touched. In the end, we are responsible for our own sense of self. We are in control.

Good health – We talked in depth about this on #11. Our minds and our bodies are intrinsically connected, so taking care of yourself from head to toe is a critical component of happiness. Whenever I am feeling below par, a long walk or workout always brings me back. Remember back niners, we don't have an option on this one.

Spirituality – Another one of our top nine components, and maybe most important of all. Regardless of your belief system, tapping into your spiritual side will certainly increase your satisfaction levels. Believing in something abundantly larger than ourselves, and identifying with how we fit into the larger scope of life is truly an awesome feeling. I speak from recent personal experience here folks, and I am happier and more fulfilled because of it.

Altruism – Giving without expectations of what you will get in return makes you feel very good about yourself. As we have already discussed, feeling good about yourself is another key to happiness. Having a positive impact on someone else's life is very rewarding, and can be very inspirational for all parties.

Perspective – Happy people typically frame their life experiences so that the good features lie in the forefront, while the bad stay in the back and out of focus. The way you look at things in your life has a direct correlation to your attitude, which we mentioned earlier. A positive outlook and perspective on life allows you take control. Reading the following words, written by Charles Swindoll, is an awesome way to help recharge the batteries if you find yourself lacking a positive attitude and proper perspective:

"The longer I live, the more I realize the impact of attitude on life. Attitude, to me is more important than facts. It is more important than the past, than education, than money, than circumstances, than failures, than success, than what other people think or say or do. It is more important than appearance, giftedness, or skill. It will make or break a company...a church...a home. The remarkable thing is we have a choice every day regarding the attitude we will

embrace for that day. We cannot change our pasts, we cannot change the fact that people will act in a certain way. We cannot change the inevitable. The only thing we can do is play on the one string we have, and that is our attitude.

I am convinced that life is 10% what happens to me and 90% how I react to it. And so it is with you – we are in charge of our attitudes."

Humor – This is one of my favorites. My favorite game I play with my children is the "kickle game." Of course, the older kids don't like it as much, but the younger ones can't get enough of my tickling. There is nothing more enjoyable to me than the laughter of my children. Even throughout my business career, I have quite often added humor to many situations, especially when the tensions are high. Humor and levity can help make very difficult circumstances more bearable, and sometimes even laughable. Make an effort to add humor and laughter to your day, and you will see your happiness meter rise.

Purpose – We discussed purpose on several golf holes on this journey, and really dug deep in the chapter on spirituality. A purpose is a personal, long-term affirmation of what you want to be. It offers lifetime direction, and it is a vital component to finding your path that leads to this purpose. Take this one seriously folks. Remember, it takes time and a deep understanding of self to discover your purpose. However, your life will be incomplete if you don't identify with this key aspect. Make some notes, state your strongest qualities, prepare a draft, and keep working on it until it's perfected. To begin to believe that you are on track to fulfilling your purpose will be the most important work you will ever do, and will lead you to a very peaceful and happy place.

Here's another exercise for you. Make a **Happiness Chart** listing these twelve components, and rate yourself on a scale of one-ten. The best possible score would be one hundred and twenty. Put the chart on your wall, and do this exercise each month for one year, starting now. As usual, I am right here with you, and contrary to some of the other projects we had encountered together, I was not very pleased this time with my results. I need some major improvements when it comes to my own Happiness. I only scored an eighty of a possible one twenty, so if this was a test in school, I would have only received a sixty seven (a D…ouch!!). I did this a few times, just to make sure I was being totally honest with myself, and sure enough, same score. That's OK; it's just another "opportunity in disguise." Even though I have a long way to go to achieve the type of true Happiness that I am looking for, I know that I am on the right path. I know that I have made tremendous progress in my life in the last few years, and I am confident that my score will increase each month. How about you? What was your score? Where do you need improvements on your Happiness chart? A very telling exercise, right?

This reminds me of another test that I took in church last week. A test I favored a bit better on than the one I just took. The series the preacher was talking about was entitled Juicy Fruit. He actually handed out packs of gum throughout the church as a reminder to keep focused of the nine juicy fruit flavors of the sprit. The message was very cool and poignant to the changes taking place in my life, and we took a test to see where we stood on these nine flavors:

Love, Joy, Peace, Patience, Kindness, Goodness, Gentleness, Faithfulness, and Self-Control.

We didn't use the same scoring criteria in church, so just to be sure I thought I would rate myself similar to the ratings on the Happiness Chart above. Go ahead, give it a try and see how you fair. The best possible score here is a ninety. Well, I scored a seventy three, which really pleased me. Using the same barometer as I did above, I would have score an eighty one on the test. There's still some room for improvement, but well on my way to living a more fruitful and spiritual life. As a matter of fact, one could safely assume that some of the Happiness criteria above could be weighted in terms of importance in our lives. Therefore, if I shifted some extra weight to Love, Spirituality, and Purpose on the Happiness Chart, my score would have increased dramatically.

OK. I am feeling better now, but how about you? How did you rate in the Juicy Fruit category? How would you weigh the Happiness criteria above? Which items are more important to you than others?

Remember, this is your back nine. You are putting together a game plan that will help you improve your life, so it's very individual to each of us. Overall, I hope you enjoyed those exercises, and I hope you can see how this all ties into our quest for true back nine happiness. Let's stay on the subject of Spirituality for a minute. For me, my renewed focus on faith has certainly led me towards a path to being more grateful, peaceful, and ultimately, happy. My vision of happiness has altered over the last few years, mostly due to the adversity I have faced. As we discussed on the prior hole, many people often find their way through the challenges they face, and when they come through on the other side, the sense of accomplishment dwarfs many of the other accomplishments from their past that were more superficial. This reminds me of the quote at the beginning of his chapter by the great Billy Graham; *it's the kind of happiness that fills our souls even in the middle of our struggles. Pure happiness that endures, not superficial happiness that is fleeting.* One could say that it would be difficult to understand this type of purity and peace if one doesn't experience a sense of hardship and struggle along the way. I really believe in this concept, as I do not know a single soul that hasn't experienced trauma in their life. It's really just a part of life. In the end, these are the times when we are truly tested. Passing these difficult tests helps us build the foundation blocks for true happiness. Like the great Confucius once said:

> *"The gem cannot be polished without friction nor the man perfected without trials."*

This was never more prevalent for me than when I was reading *The Shack,* by William Paul Young. The unbelievable tragedy and pain that the main character experienced in this book was almost unbearable. Ultimately, this pain led him down a path to truly find himself, and he was confronted with the unique opportunity to ask God a series of questions that had gone unanswered for years. What he found was a sense of joy and happiness that he had never had before in his life, and it all came as a result of the most unspeakable horror one could imagine. You see, it's the "uncommon" things in life where the true lessons are learned, which is another lesson that I learned from reading Tony Dungy's book of the same name, *Uncommon*.

One could say that it is more common to take the easy way out, to live selfishly, to have tunnel vision, and to let material possessions and impressing people take over your life. I can speak from personal experience, these things DO NOT lead to Happiness. They lead you to a cold, dark, and lonely place. On the other hand, if you choose the "road less traveled" or the "uncommon" approach to life centered in faith, enlightenment, and positivity...your road to Happiness will become crystal clear.

Similar to the seven principles of golf we outlined to get our bearings set for some improvements in our lives on the last hole, Dungy outlines seven principles of his own in this great book. You see, there are many different paths to Happiness, and Dungy's book outlines a more spiritual and simple path. Notice the similarities between this list and our Happiness Chart.

Here are his seven principles:

- **Develop Your Core** – Character, Honesty and Integrity, Humility and Stewardship, Courage
- **Love Your Family** – How to Treat a Woman, Fatherhood, Respect Authority
- **Lift Your Friends and Others** – Friendship, Taking Council, The Power of Positive Influence, Mentoring
- **Your Full Potential** – Powerful Thought, Education and Athletics, Career, Alcohol and Drugs, Failure
- **Establish A Mission That Matters** – Style versus Substance, Priorities, Being versus Doing, Creating Balance
- **Choose Influence Over Image** – Respect Yourself and Others, Sexual Integrity, Role Model
- **Live Your Faith** – Eternal Self-Esteem Relationship with Christ, Faith, Purpose, Significance

Every single one of our nine key components to life is outlined in this book. Family, Health, Knowledge, Career, Spirituality, Leadership, Relationships, Self Improvement, and of course, Happiness. This is great, we are so on our way to creating an awesome **back nine**. Can you feel it?

> *Back on the course. Solid tee shot, again. Your ball has landed safely on the green, and you are about 30 feet from the pin. You have another chance at birdie on this finishing hole. Your putting stroke has been phenomenal on the last few holes, so draw upon that as you try and make your last putt. Get your line, get your stance, and stroke it firmly!*

Stroke 2 – Authenticity - The "Mirror Check"

"There once was a very cautious man, Who never laughed or cried, He never cared, he never dared, He never dreamed or tried, And when one day he passed away, His insurance was denied, For since he never really lived, They claimed he never died"

— Author Unknown

OK, so we have learned a great deal about ourselves over the course of this journey. Our challenge now, is to put all we have learned into play in real time, in real life. If we truly want to be happy in our hearts, we have to take one last long look, a look in the mirror. I used to use this phrase all of the time. The folks that have worked with me who are reading this book probably have a smile on their face at this very moment. With the "**mirror check,**" you take a close look at yourself to really see if you are doing the right things. Are you being true to yourself? Are you living the life you thought you should be living? Are you honest with yourself and others? Are you living an authentic life? When I first started this project, the answers to all of these questions for me, was NO. Imagine having to live with yourself when you are a person that was constantly telling others that they need to be conducting "mirror checks" on themselves when all along you never really did them on yourself? Well, that was me, the "Old Tony."

Someone asked me the other day, "Family tragedies aside, what do you fear most?" I said that my biggest fear was to NOT live authentically. To NOT be able to live to my full capacity. To NOT be able to live all of the things I am writing in this book.

That is my biggest fear. That I will drift back into a life of sin, self-serving, and egomania. A life filled with gambling, womanizing, drinking, drug abuse, etc.... You see, I am quite confident that I will be financially secure, again, at some point in the near future. When this happens, then my ultimate test will really begin. Can I live more authentically when I have the means to go back to feeding my demons? It's kind of easy now, because I do not have the means to do the things I used to do. Well, I shouldn't say easy, because my life has certainly not been easy the last few years. Will I be able to keep my natural zest for life, yet stay true to my faith, my children, my soul? Bottom line, this is what I fear the most. What is it that you fear? What are your demons? What are the things that you need to avoid that will halt your progress to Happiness?

Be honest, write them down. Now is the time to settle of this stuff, before we begin to truly LIVE our lives. Now is the time to let this stuff go, to put it down, and to really find our true and authentic selves.

I have some more good news for you when it comes to authenticity. If you have been struggling with this in your life, the good news is that you really don't have to search very far. It's already in you, from birth. We are all born authentic, we live our childhoods in a pure and authentic manner, and God made each of us to be authentic. All we have to do is "remember." Sort of like our authentic golf swing we have been talking about throughout this book. As Bagger Vance says in Steven Pressfield's masterpiece:

> *"I believe that each of us possesses, inside ourselves, one true Authentic Swing that is ours alone. It is a folly to try and teach us another, or mold us to some ideal version of the perfect swing. Each player possesses only that one swing that he was born with, that swing which existed within him before he ever picked up a club. Like the statue of David, our Authentic Swing already exists, concealed within stone, so to speak. Our task as golfers is simply to chip away all that is*

inauthentic, allowing our Authentic Swing to emerge in its purity."

There is beauty is this statement beyond words. A beauty and pureness that has captivated me for some time, and has been part of the inspiration for this entire endeavor. I watched this movie, *The Legend of Bagger Vance* for the second time last year, just a few days before I awoke in the middle of the night with the vision for this book. The connection between life and golf, and more importantly, the connection between the search for our Authentic Swings and the search for our Authentic Self (or soul) is the single most important concept of our back nine journey. I have put together a list of nine life components for us to work on, in an attempt to get right here, right now, back to our Authentic Self. This is the child within each and every one of us that is just dying to be unleashed. The purest form of who we are, the shape that God intended for us at birth, that we lost sight of somewhere along the way. This movie (and book) has infused its way into my being. I have since read the book twice and watched the movie a half-dozen times. Just again, last night, in preparation for this golf shot. Bagger Vance goes on to say:

"This game of golf is a metaphor for the soul's search for its true ground and identity.

We enter onto this material plane, not in utter nakedness, but trailing clouds of glory do we come from God, who is our home. In other words, already possessing a highly refined and individual soul. Our job here is to recall that soul and become it. To form a union with it, a yoga, as they say in India. In the East, men are not embarrassed to speak openly of the Self. But here in the West, such piety makes people uncomfortable. That is where golf comes in. The search for the Authentic Swing is parallel to the search for the Self. We as golfers pursue that elusive essence our entire lives. What hooks us about the game is that it gives us glimpses. Glimpses of the Authentic Swing, like the mystic being granted a vision of the face of God. All we need to do is experience it once

– one mid-iron screaming like a bullet toward the flag, one drive flushed down the middle – and we're enslaved forever. We feel the absolute certainty that if we could only swing like that all of the time, we would be our best selves, our true selves, our authentic selves."

The "essence" of our lives, I love that statement. What is the essence of your life? What swing changes are you willing to make to ensure your back nine will be the best it can be? Like I mentioned above, thanks to God, we already possess a highly refined and individual soul. We already possess our one true and authentic swing (self). So, how do we tap into it, and how do we remember what it looks like? Well, we have to trust ourselves again. We have done so much work throughout this journey, and have uncovered so many key aspects of our lives. Now, all we have to do is trust that we can live the way we want. We have to execute our game plan. We must realize that we already have all of the answers; they already reside inside our minds.

We each have special talents, special abilities, all given to us by God. We have the knowledge. Now, it's up to us to transform that knowledge into energy, that energy into action, and that action into health, hope, freedom, and Happiness. This is not just a way of thinking about life; it is a way of LIVING life. Time to let go of your insecurities and your self-limiting beliefs that have been ingrained in you for years. Time to disassociate yourself from your circumstances and your pain. Time to realize that you and you alone, are responsible for your own back nine happiness. You see, for many of us, there is a huge gap between knowing and doing. Tony Dungy refers to it above as being versus doing.

It's all about doing the things that we know are right, especially when the easy choice involves doing the things that we know are wrong. We have talked in depth about discipline throughout these golf holes, and here it is again. We just have to make up our minds to change. Than we must stick with it and stay "steadfast and strong" while we continue down our path. The worst thing we can do is start something and then quit. This will only break the pact we have made with ourselves. We must first honor the promises that we make to ourselves before we can honor any other promises. We must practice what we preach. A lesson that I have learned the hard way, but I am thankful to have learned it all. Remember, contrary to what others may say on this topic, it is truly never too late. We must stay completely FOCUSED. This is another word that I have used often throughout my career, and will bring another smile to the faces of those who have worked with me in the past.

To help me stay focused on my personal back nine journey, I made up an acronym for FOCUS. I do this quite often with words that I love, because it helps me stay dialed into the meaning behind the word. This word has special meaning for me, as I'm sure it does for many. You see, focused energy is like a laser beam. You can bask in sun rays for hours, but if you harness the pure energy of laser beam rays, you can burn through solid steel. This is the kind of focus we will need to accomplish our **back nine** goals, my friends. Here's my acronym for **FOCUS**:

F – Fitness
O – One day at a time
C – Clean (minimize mistakes…learn from mistakes)
U – Unselfish
S – Strength

Another critical component to ensure **back nine** happiness will be **FAITH**. I have also created an acronym for faith that helps in the same manner.

F – Fatherhood
A – Attitude
I – Identity
T – Truth
H – Humble

Have some fun with these, and make up your own. Keep them posted to your wall in your office or at home, and use them as reminders to keep the FAITH and to stay FOCUSED. As you will notice, the reminders I that use have more to do with other components of my life, rather than the actual words of Faith and Focus. This way, I can utilize the POWER of those words, not only to help me with faith and focus, but to help me in other aspects of my life. What I have found is that nothing is too corny, especially if it helps me accomplish my goals, which is what we are all after, right?

Here's another exercise that may help. Make a new chart that includes all nine key life components, and tape it to your wall. Give yourself a score and than rate yourself each month, quarter, or year. It's a great way to chart your overall progress as you pave the path to your ultimate back nine.

- Family
- Health and Wellness
- Knowledge
- Career
- Spirituality
- Leadership
- Relationships
- Self Improvement
- Happiness

I have not scored myself yet, but plan to start soon. This will actually be taped to the mirror in my bathroom, which is a place that is personal and a place that I really can't fool anyone. I can't fool myself in the mirror and I can't fool God.

Back on the course. *I knew it, another great putt, and another birdie. That is a birdie, birdie, finish. Unbelievable. Your progress on this* **back nine** *has been nothing short of a miracle. Your final score...32...or 4 under par. 5 pars and 4 birdies, a phenomenal achievement, and one that you will not soon forget.*

OK, let's go the 19th hole and celebrate!!!!

The 19ᵗʰ Hole (conclusion)

After a round of golf it is customary to join your playing partners in the clubhouse for some refreshments, discussion, and reflection. These conversations usually are centered on the round that you just played. The shot you hit on #15, the putt you missed on #12, and a ton of discussion about your overall game and score. Well, our focus here on our 19ᵗʰ hole will be similar. We will talk about what we just experienced, what we plan on doing next time we play, and draw upon some key reference points throughout the back nine that will help us carve out improvements for the rest of our lives.

We just got through playing nine grueling golf holes together, and we finished with a back nine score of **32**(there is that number again). We uncovered many important items that will help improve our lives. Now, it's time for us to put these into play, and to work hard in an attempt to grow each day. However, it's important to remember, that this will take time. Our back nine journey will last the rest of our lives, and it's not something that we should ever step back from and admire because we feel it's complete. It will never be complete, and our journey will continue to be loaded with struggle, disappointment, and failure.

It's so awesome that we have learned so much about ourselves throughout this journey, because the knowledge and insight we have gained will give us a better chance of handling our adversity. Our improvements will include an ongoing process of building, refining, renovating, and practicing. If you ever have trouble staying patient on your back nine (which many of us do), remember The Cathedral

Principle. The magnificent Cathedrals in Europe, built centuries ago, very often took several lifetimes to build and construct. They obviously couldn't be erected like the buildings of today. They took generations to build. Remember, one of our main goals during our time on this earth is to construct something that will be sustainable when we are gone, and to leave the world a better place then we found it. You are actually that important, and the things that you do will have a lasting impact on the world (and the people) you leave behind. Our goal is not to get it right; our goal is to continue to work on improvements. Our goal is to do our best to not make the same mistakes that plagued us on the front nine of our lives. Regardless of your age, the positive changes that you make today will help you secure the back nine of your dreams. They will help you with your family relationships, improve your health, continue your quest for knowledge, transform your career, keep you focused on spirituality, improve your ability to cultivate relationships, stay dialed into self-improvement, and ultimately guide you into a more happy and fulfilling life.

What an awesome opportunity we have to make our lives better and it's an opportunity that not everyone gets. Many people never get to live out their back nine dreams, and still others make a mess out of their back nine, many of whom had a fantastic and privileged front nine. To illustrate my point on these two extremes, I will be assisted by the number **32**. I told you we would come back to this number, and it will become clear as to why in a few moments.

This was my favorite number when I was a kid. As I mentioned earlier on a few occasions, I was a huge sports fan when I was a young boy. Playing sports for me provided an early glimpse into what authenticity is all about. I was on my true path back then, and this is the feeling I will try and duplicate as I live my back nine. I didn't play golf as a kid, but I played almost every other sport. I first wore the number **32** in basketball, because my favorite player at the time, Dr. J (Julius Erving) wore that number for the New York Nets. Yes, they were first the New York Nets (before they moved to NJ), and they played on Long Island where I grew up. They played in the ABA, which was the "flashier" version of the NBA and it was very exciting to watch. Especially Dr J, with his smooth moves, high flying and dunking, he immediately became my favorite player. Over the years, basketball was always my favorite sport, and while I was in high school, my second favorite basketball player came on the scene. His name was Magic Johnson, and he also wore number **32**. The number **32** stuck with me throughout my sports playing years, although the number wasn't as readily available in other sports, like soccer. But it was in football, when I was inspired by another famous number **32** that reinforced my affinity for this number. His name was O.J. Simpson. I was a huge fan of O.J. Simpson when I was a kid. He played football with a combination of style, grace, and toughness, and I was mesmerized by his on the field excellence. I even enjoyed watching O.J. doing his Hertz TV commercials, as well as his performances in the *Police Squad* series. Well, as with many of his former fans, my love affair with O.J. ended as soon as I watch him flee police in his white Ford Bronco in 1994. Interestingly enough, I was **32** at the time. As I described above, some people get to lead very privileged and fruitful front nine's, and O.J. Simpson was a prime example. This man was blessed with everything, yet he threw it all away, and will probably never have the opportunity to truly find himself. Although he was amazingly acquitted of the original murder charges, he was finally brought to justice last year, and in my opinion, is finally where he belongs…in jail.

Let's switch gears for a minute and talk about another sports figure. At the age of **32**, the late Payne Stewart won his first major golf championship, the 1989 PGA Championship. I talked about Payne and the book I read about his life in the spirituality chapter. This man and this book have had a tremendous impact on me and my life. I never met Payne, but I can definitely identify with the changes that took place in his life. Unfortunately, ten years after his 1989 PGA victory, his life was cut short in a tragic plane crash. But unlike the situation above with Mr. Simpson, Payne Stewart had already found his path and started his authentic back nine journey. He had already faced his demons, came full circle, and recommitted his life to his family and his faith. The year he died, 1999, was an incredible year for Payne Stewart. Not only did he win the U.S. Open, he also was a member of the Ryder Cup team who came back from a daunting deficit to defeat the Europeans in Brookline, Mass. I was at the 18th

hole at Pinehurst, North Carolina, when Payne sunk a fifteen foot putt to win the 1999 US Open for the second time (he also won in 1991).

I have a framed picture hanging in my office, that I am looking at right now, that is entitled, *"One moment in Time"*. I can remember that moment like it was yesterday. The roar of the crowd was deafening, and my ears were ringing for days. I was so excited for Payne, as I was always a huge fan.

It's funny, because he actually beat one of my other favorite golfers, Phil Michelson, on that famed last hole. But it's what happened on that final green, something that I didn't know at the time, that solidified this man's legacy for me. Let me just give you a glimpse into the type of man that Payne Stewart turned out to be. After his miraculous putt to win the 1999 U.S. Open, he walked over to Phil (who was expecting his first child), put his hands around Phil's face, and told him that what he was getting ready to experience (fatherhood) was going to be the most spectacular event of his life. This guy just won the U.S. Open, the crowd was going crazy, yet he had the presence of mind to acknowledge the "life situation" of his opponent. To this day, even as I write this, I get chills down my spine. You see, Payne Stewart knew what life was about, and he knew that there was a higher calling, beyond golf, and even beyond himself. That is what the back nine is all about, my friends.

In the end, our lives are what we make them. It may sound cliché, but we do have a choice. A choice to live our back nine with determination and focus on who we want to be, what we want to achieve, and what significant contributions we want to leave behind. A choice to continue our search for our one, true, and totally authentic selves. The authentic selves that God made us to be, in his image, and to take advantage of all of the tools he has bestowed upon us and our lives. A choice to stop making excuses for what has happened to us, and to take responsibility and move on with a strong and steady demeanor.

It's a continuing process and we must remember that we are here for just a very short time. Our life is truly a temporary assignment, but it can be spectacular, fulfilling, and wonderful all the same. We must continue to possess hindsight, foresight, and insight as we set out to capture all that life has to offer. We mush continue to live in the present, enjoy each day, and not think too much about the past nor long for the future.

Our moment is now, and our day is today.

"It is the soul that makes a man rich. He is rich or poor according to what he is and not according to what he has"

—Henry Ward Beecher

Acknowledgements

I would like to thank all of the people that have helped me throughout the process of writing *My Back Nine*. It has been an incredible two year journey, and I feel blessed to be aided by so many phenomenal individuals.

Cindy Valliere, my life coach turned close friend, who was there for me in my time of need. Your initial assessments, advice, positive and direct attitude, and overall friendship helped me get started on this two year endeavor, and I am eternally grateful. *Alice Osborn*, my editor, who did an awesome job providing writing advice, editing, and guidance. *Jane Blaise Fay*, my very talented niece, who's artwork elevated the authenticity of this project.

My incredible bevy of close friends throughout the country (*you know who you are*) that have been so supportive of me throughout this process. Your encouraging words through phone calls and e-mails helped fuel the fire within as I paved my way through the pages of *My back Nine*. I can't express the importance of each of these individual relationships, and I feel privileged to have so many supporters and close friends in my life.

My parents, *Nick and Barbara Caico*, who have been there for me my entire life. Especially, *YOU mom*. Your trust, confidence, unconditional love, and belief in me have always there regardless of the circumstances.

Finally, to *AJ, Austin, Alexander, Andersen, and Annalise*, who inspire me every day to be the best that I can be. It's comforting to know that I will have a built-in foursome for the rest of my playing days.

About the Author

Tony Caico is an accomplished sales executive, manager, speaker and presenter. He has been in sales and sales management for over twenty five years, and has experienced a great deal of success in several industries. He started his career in the tire and auto industry, moved into mortgage banking, and most recently has entered a more entrepreneurial phase of his life as a writer, speaker, and consultant.

Caico is also an avid golfer. He has been playing this awesome game for over two decades, and has had the privilege of playing some of the great courses throughout the country. He truly enjoys everything the sport has to offer, especially now that golf has provided the last piece of adhesive needed to capture his overall message. As he cites in the pages of *My Back Nine*, his golf game is a mirror image of his personality, and it has improved as he has improved. His passion for golf combined with his passion for business, writing, and connecting with people, proved to be the grout in the tiles for *My Back Nine*.

Caico lives in Durham, North Carolina. He is the proud father of five incredible children; A.J., Austin, Alexander, Andersen, and Annalise.

References:

The Father's Almanac, by S. Adams Sullivan

The Legend of Bagger Vance, by Steven Pressfield

Raising a SON, by Don and Jean Elium

YOU: The Owner's Manual, by Michael F. Roizen and Mehmet C. Oz

YOU: On a Diet, by Michael F. Roizen and Mehmet

The Seven Principles of Golf, by Darrin Gee

The Intellectual Devotional, by Kidder & Oppenheim

Uncommon, by Tony Dungy

Golf is not a Game of Perfect, by Bob Rotella

Wins, Losses, and Lessons, by Lou Holtz

The Power of Now, by Eckart Tolle

Payne Stewart, by Tracey Stewart

The 21 Irrefutable Qualities of a Leader, John Maxwell

The 360 Leader, John Maxwell

The Little Black Book of Connections, Jeffery Gittomer

The Sales Bible, by Jeffery Gittomer

A Purpose Driven Life, Rick Warren

Put Your Dreams to the Test, by John Maxwell

Excuses Be Gone, by Dr. Wayne Dyer

Strength Finder 2.0, by Dan Rath

The Shack, by W.M. Paul Young

Golf for Enlightenment, by Deepak Chopra

Leadership Primer, by Colin Powell